DOMINATORS

Of

COMMERCIAL REAL ESTATE

BROKERAGE

ROD SANTOMASSIMO

CCIM

DOMINATORS

Of

COMMERCIAL REAL ESTATE

BROKERAGE

ROD SANTOMASSIMO

CCIM

TABLE OF CONTENTS

Acknowledgments

This book is dedicated to my writing partner, Wally Bock. Over the past two years, Wally and I have dealt with issues neither of us expected nor wanted. Wally, always my guide, took on a bigger role than we anticipated. Wally is a business writer who dominates.

PREFACE

I wrote the first draft of *Commercial Real Estate Brokers Who DOMINATE – The 8 Traits of Top Producers* in 2011. It was my first book, and I had a simple objective. I would share the best practices of some of North America's most prolific CRE agents.

The Great Recession ravaged transaction velocity from 2008 – 2010. For most in the industry, it was the lowest economic point of their careers. Many left the industry entirely. Others packed up their desks and worked from home until conditions improved. But there were some brokers who adapted and widened the gap between themselves and their lower-producing peers. They dominated.

DOMINATE is an acronym.

Brokers Who Dominate
are **D**isciplined,
are **O**riented to their client,
have a strong **M**arket presence,
are **I**ndustry specialists,
Navigate their careers,
are **A**ssertive,
are **T**eam oriented, and
are **E**ntrepreneurial.

The original book was published in 2012. It became the first of three best-sellers and remains my overall best-selling book. In fact, "Brokers Who DOMINATE," as it is commonly referred to, remains one of the most-sold commercial real estate brokerage books of all time. It also signaled the emergence of the Massimo Group.

Ten years ago, the Massimo Group was myself, a couple of new coaches, and my admin, Maggie Williams. We were not "dominant" in any way, shape or form. However, ten years later, we have served thousands of commercial real estate coaching clients, whom we refer to as our Massimo Members. Our services have expanded to assist every success, experience, and budget level. Our programs are guaranteed based on the incredible success of our clients.

Today, we have 35 Certified Massimo CRE coaches, which is growing. In addition, we have a complete leadership team, including Maggie, who is now our Director of Member Success.

In 2016, in my second book, *Commercial Real Estate Teams Built to DOMINATE,* I shared how some of the industry's top-producing teams are structured and the practices they use to create a winning culture and consistently high commissions. The lessons I learned from writing that book would become critically important only a few years later.

When I started thinking about writing a 10th-anniversary book for Brokers Who DOMINATE, I did not expect us to face a far worse downturn than the Great Recession. Beyond the tragic loss of life, the Pandemic of 2020 created a complete lockdown in the commercial real estate industry as we knew it. At least, that's how it seemed to many observers.

When everything was seemingly crumbling around us, clients reached out to the dominant CRE brokers for clarity and comfort. Those dominant brokers developed alternatives, options, and solutions for property owners and users who believed the only solution was to close shop.

Today, the Massimo Group is the world's dominant commercial real estate broker/agent coaching company. We have learned to adapt as well.

We had to adapt in 2020 to help our commercial real estate coaching clients get some clarity on how to work with their clients, and how to quickly take on the position of a resource versus a transactor if they had not already. We helped them navigate Payroll Protection Plans (PPP). We brought in tax strategists and program experts to help our clients understand the various stimulus packages' impact on them and their clients.

Today, with the recent development of Artificial Intelligence platforms, we are again leading the way by showing brokers how to leverage this new technology. We are also integrating AI into all our coaching programs.

Our goal was to help our clients thrive in the new CRE world. As the writing of this book, Massimo Group coaching clients are coming off their most productive year in our history, having closed over $24.6 Billion in transaction volume last year.

I wrote this book because the brokers who DOMINATE have more lessons to teach us all. The traits I identified in 2011 are still potent guides to success. The lessons from *Teams Built to DOMINATE* still work in the age of the hybrid workplace. This book adds insights from a decade filled with challenges that dominant brokers met with insights and creativity, and some ideas about what lies ahead for CRE.
I wish you good reading and great success!

Rod Santomassimo
June 2023

INTRODUCTION

"If I have seen further, it is by standing on the shoulders of giants."

Isaac Newton said that in a letter to Robert Hooke in 1675. He attributed much of his success to what he learned from others who went before him. That's the spirit behind my first and best-selling book, Brokers Who DOMINATE, and my second book, Teams Built to Dominate.

I wrote those books to share what top CRE pros had figured out so that readers like you could learn from them and improve. This book is filled with lessons those same pros can teach us today- after one of the most tumultuous decades our business has ever been through.

I reached out to every individual and team I wrote about in my first two books. Some did not respond in time to be included in this book. Others are now in different roles than brokerage but still in the industry. Brad Ahrens is running a very successful development and investment company. Tim Strange is focusing on orchestrating investments as well. One of those profiled, Ms. Faith Consolo, passed away in December 2018. "You Got to Have Faith!" is a personal brand I will never forget.

In Brokers Who DOMINATE, I divided those I profiled into three groups. The "Young Guns" had four to seven years of experience but showed great promise. They've continued to find their own way in the business and innovate. For the last fourteen years, Jill Duemeland has been in the office an average of three days a week and has never been there five days in a row. You'll find out how she does it.

Most of the brokers I profiled in Brokers Who DOMINATE, and those in Teams Built to Dominate were in the midst of their careers when I wrote those books. They continued their successful ways even when the pandemic seemed to upend the world for everyone else. They came up with ways to support their clients and found opportunities they could seize in the crisis.

Brent Miller initiated and ran a weekly virtual meeting with the Mayor of Salisbury, community leaders, and elected officials to inform the community about how the pandemic affected the business community. Bob Knakal took advantage of the business slowdown to drive and walk every single block of Manhattan south of 9th Street, logging every building under construction and every potential development site.

Game Changers were the third group in Brokers Who DOMINATE. Game Changers are brokers who have literally designed the way our current brokerage business works. In 2011 I wrote, "You would be wrong to assume these are in the twilight of their careers. All three would tell you they have a long way to go and much more to do."

Well, in 2023, they're all still active and you'll find out what they're up to today. The chapter on Jerry Anderson leads off the book, and Stephen Siegel's is the last chapter in this book. They share their thoughts on the business based on their combined 100+ years of experience.

In the chapter on Jerry Anderson, you'll hear him compare the effects of the pandemic to the Tax Reform Act of 1986. In Stephen Siegel's chapter, you'll learn why he would recommend that his children consider a career in commercial real estate. Between those two chapters, there are nineteen other chapters filled with wisdom, ideas and examples you can use to boost your own career.

THE BASICS STILL MATTER

In case you're wondering, the basics still matter. The brokers profiled here conform to the DOMINATE theme outlined in my first book. Specifically, they are:

Disciplined
Oriented to the Client
Market Presence
Industry/geography focus
Navigate careers
Assertive
Team oriented
Efficient

Despite many changes in our business, those activities continue to generate success. That's why they're still the core of our coaching. As Dr. Michael LeBeouf said, "The great truths are too important to be new."

Let's take one example: prospecting. Most brokers dislike prospecting. Few do it well, and many try to avoid it. The giants profiled in this book embrace prospecting as a key to their success.

Bob Knakal will tell you that nothing is more important than having a great prospecting plan and setting aside the time to implement it. He sets aside a minimum of eight hours per week for prospecting calls and schedules prospecting time two weeks in advance.

In Bob's chapter, you'll learn about his new prospecting approach. Yes, after decades of the kind of success many brokers only dream of, Bob Knakal still thinks prospecting is central to his success and he's still working to do it better.

He's not alone. The Coppola-Cheney Group has developed a way to turn cold calling into a competitive event. Brad Umansky is discovering ways to use social media to support his firm's prospecting and presence-building efforts. Throughout this book, you'll find ways to improve the way you do the basics.

In addition to the basics, four themes emerged as I reviewed all the responses. They're not "new" or even particularly related to the last decade. They're insights from successful and experienced brokers that help us understand how to deliver on the basics today.

DELIVER VALUE TO YOUR CLIENTS

Being oriented to your client is important, but as Jerry Anderson points out, brokers who dominate bring more value. When you deliver more value, your client is willing to pay more because they get more. Very often that "more" goes beyond the basic transaction. The brokers in this book are constantly looking for ways to deliver more value to their clients.

Caulley Deringer sums up the "how" this way: "My team pushes themselves to 'think' like our clients, which allows us a more meaningful understanding of their business goals which has us uniquely aligned with them as partners, rather than clients." In Caulley's chapter, you'll find more about how his team delivers value by customizing their approach to every client.

The pandemic offered many brokers opportunities to provide value to their clients. You find an excellent example of delivering value during the pandemic in Mark Myer's chapter. Mark specializes in senior housing properties of all types, and the pandemic challenged him and his clients in unique ways.

Here's one example. Nursing homes and other senior care facilities faced a Personal Protective Equipment (PPE) shortage. So, Mark and his team helped them connect with vendors of PPE and other disease-control items. They also helped their clients by sharing good ideas and best practices from other similar facilities.

Here's another way to deliver value. Matt McGregor and Bill Condon stepped back to view the real estate transaction as a cog in a client's supply chain. They discovered several ways in which the real estate decision can affect value for the client because real estate costs only account for +/- 6% of the actual cost of the location. The team's supply chain analytics service adds huge value for clients and a competitive advantage for the team.

STRONG PROCESSES AND HABITS MAKE SUCCESS HAPPEN

Jill Duemeland could be the poster child for the phrase "work smarter, not harder." Over the last fourteen years, she's been in the office an average of three days per week while building a growing and successful brokerage. In her chapter, Jill lists her three secrets of success. Number 2 is "Processes."

The classic definition of a process is "a series of steps or actions that are taken to achieve a specific outcome." The outcome might be obtaining a new client or completing a transaction. Other outcomes are administrative, like hiring a new team member. When you have strong processes and follow them, everyone will do the same steps in the same order every time.

You may associate "processes" with giant three-ring binders filled with pages of tiny type. It doesn't have to be that way. Back to Jill, again. In her chapter, you'll learn a simple way to create processes for your business.

Kyle Nagy says that he invests in "People, Process, and Technology." Technology is key since many of today's processes are enshrined in software. Many chapters in this book outline the way a particular broker has leveraged technology and processes to improve operations.

A habit is "a behavior that is repeated regularly, often unconsciously." James Nelson describes how they work this way:

"To achieve a goal, you must define what the goal is. Then you must create a plan to achieve that goal. So far, so good. Now develop habits that define what you must do every day to work that plan."

Ken Ashley is another broker who talked about habits. Here's what he said about why you should pay attention to yours.

"Don't underestimate the power of habits and rituals. Motivation is an emotion, and emotions come and go. Habits tend to get acted on no matter how you feel."

Processes and habits will help you dominate in two ways. First, they assure the consistency that efficiency is based on. Plus, when you have processes and habits working for you, you don't need to reinvent action steps every time. Instead, you can use all your cognitive capacity on the creative aspects of the work.

PLAY THE LONG GAME AND KEEP IMPROVING

The greatest lesson (among many) that Jerry Anderson taught me is that commercial real estate success is a long-term achievement and requires a long-term perspective. The brokers profiled in this book have learned that lesson.

More than a decade ago, Marshall Goldsmith wrote a book titled *What Got You Here Won't Get You There: How Successful People Become Even More Successful.* You don't have to read it to take the title to heart. It's the essence of how the brokers in this book understand personal improvement.

Pay attention to your inputs. Are you reading material that will help you grow and improve? Or are you stuffing your brain with Netflix series, SportsCenter, and dubious social media experts? It's up to you. Learn from the example of the brokers in this book, like Bo Barron who says, "I read at least one book per week, and I'm striving to learn from others' successes and failures. These lessons I pass on to my team and we implement them into our business."

Matt McGregor suggests an ambitious target in his chapter. He thinks you should strive to stay about twelve months ahead of the curve. Then, you can advise your clients on what's coming and not just how to react to what's already happened.

James Nelson says you should never stop learning. In his chapter, you'll read about how things were going well, and he thought he didn't need a coach. He thought he could figure it all out on his own and wound up on what I call "the transaction treadmill." Looking back James says, "If you don't have a coach and mentors who are pushing you out of your comfort zone, you can't make quantum leaps in your business and life."

Tuning up your brain is only part of the long game. You must keep improving your business and finding ways to improve things. Kyle Nagy has a sign in a prominent place in his office that says, "The Restless Pursuit of Improvement." Other brokers may not have a sign, but they're constantly coming up with new ways to do things. Here are just a few examples.

Sam DiFranco has developed his "Speed to Cash" system and Mark Myers created his "Minimum Bid Strategy." Matt McGregor's team has their "Sequential 7-Step Prospecting Pursuit Process" and Ken Ashley developed his "Pivot Model" for helping his team be as productive as possible. Those processes and innovations have names. Most don't. You'll find at least one good idea in every chapter.

LONG TERM SUCCESS IS BUILT ON RELATIONSHIPS

With all the emphasis on techniques and technology, you may be forgiven if you think they're the most important drivers of long-term success. But you'd be wrong. Transactions may appear to be the most important thing, but solid, long-term relationships drive transactions and long-term success.

You'll read that message from Jerry Anderson in the first chapter of this book, and you'll see it in action in Stephen Siegel's chapter that ends the book. In between, you'll find that advice in chapter after chapter, including a description of how Bruce Lauer builds relationships and long-term clients.

Now, it's time to get started. If you want to triple your learning experience, read the original, corresponding chapter from either of the two original DOMINATE books and then read the profile in this book. Beyond the history lesson, you will learn 3x the number of winning approaches to finding and winning business.

Are you ready to stand on the shoulders of giants?

Grab a pen and a notebook, perhaps your Remarkable or iPad, depending on how you are consuming this document. Climb up on the shoulders of these giants and get ready to learn.

Have intellectual curiosity and implement. Because, as my third book shared, "Knowing Isn't Doing". Don't KID yourself and think just listening or reading this book will change your commercial real estate business trajectory. It won't. But if you apply what you learn, then you will grow, and soon you too will be in a position to be a commercial real estate broker who DOMINATES.

DOMINATORS
IN
ACTION

JERRY ANDERSON, CCIM
THE MENTOR MOVES ON

There comes a time when everyone eventually throttles back. No one I know deserves this more than Jerry Anderson, CCIM, who has been assisting clients and firms in building their wealth through Commercial Real Estate for over five decades. His client list includes some of the world's most respected institutions and CRE brokerage firms. Jerry is proud to have been a CCIM instructor for 20 years and estimates that he has trained over 20,000 CRE professionals.

In May 1997, Jerry spent a month at Mt. Everest basecamp and climbed into the Khumbu Ice Fall. He's climbed many mountains in his life, physical mountains and business mountains. So, if we ever get a Mount Rushmore for commercial real estate brokerage, Jerry's face will surely be there. And if Jerry had any say on its location, it would be on a beach in Florida or in the western North Carolina mountains.

Over the last 15 years, at the "tail-end" of his 50-year career, Jerry developed the state of Florida for SVN International Commercial Real Estate Advisors. He attracted and now mentors over 20 Florida offices in the SVN system. They have earned hundreds of millions of dollars in commissions delivering a high level of service to occupiers and owners of commercial real estate.

The high activity velocity creates a high revenue volume year after year for SVN and Jerry. But Jerry's contract with the SVN franchisor expired right before this book was published. And understandably, SVN wanted a bigger piece of the FL brokerage pie. That's ok with Jerry. He admits, "It's time," and says, "I have several opportunities that have caught my eye!"

Imagine you are in your mid 70's and think you've seen everything commercial real estate brokerage can throw at you. You've faced deal successes and failures, unrealistic sellers, impossible buyers, difficult attorneys, administration changes, tax law changes, terrorist attacks, stock market crashes, a roller coaster of interest rates, zoning issues, the rise of the internet, and a worldwide pandemic.

The impact of any one of these events by themselves can sidetrack and disrupt a career, but Jerry adapted and is still standing. And it would be foolish to think that Jerry won't be doing consulting work for CRE companies and advisors for years to come.

THE LAST TEN YEARS

Over the last ten years since Brokers Who DOMINATE was published, Jerry has leveraged all the skills, knowledge, and relationships he acquired over his long tenure as a CRE advisor. But he says, "For me, the last ten years of my career have been basically benefiting from work that I have already done." In other words, now that he built out the State of Florida, his life is slower.

Jerry is more like a coach than anything else at this point. When SVN franchisees and advisors in Florida have questions, they come to him. The questions cover finding and winning business, brokerage conflicts, client obstacles, individual pipeline growth struggles, and more.

One of Jerry's most impactful accomplishments over the last decade has been his ability to attract firms to join SVN in Florida. Think about the fierce competition for top-performing brokers and small brokerage firms. Everyone is coming after you with offers and promises, yet Jerry somehow won more than his fair share for SVN without offering signing bonuses.

Anderson's secret is that his recruiting plan is no different from his established broker prospecting plan. Jerry describes it this way.

"First off, I remove the word recruit from my vocabulary, so this is no different from working to win an assignment. I had a lot of touchpoints. Whenever I saw a deal close for a particular firm I was targeting, I would reach out to the procuring broker. I would send them a note of congratulations, mostly electronically, but occasionally I'd do it by hand and a follow-up phone call."

You may think this is old-fashioned. Think again. Over the most recent 36 months, Jerry brought on five firms to join SVN in Florida, which now, in the aggregate, generate over $50M in gross commissions annually.

As Jerry shared, "These successful entities are not firms one recruits. You get to know them, discover their 'points of business pain,' and offer a few valuable suggestions to relieve that pain. Then, if their interest rises to a lukewarm temperature, I ask, 'Who else in the marketplace should I be talking to? Our national clients need assistance in your market, and your local firm would fit well into a top ten CRE platform like SVN.' That was always the open-ended question that stimulated serious conversation."

How does this relate to prospecting? Well, Jerry would say it's no different than cold calling. After years of cold calling, Jerry says he realized cold calling is not his style. Every time he saw an article, every time he saw a lot cleared or a new building going up, he would reach out to the owner with a note and say, "Hey, I saw your activity at the corner of 4th and Main Street, that's really exciting. Next time I'm close by, I'd love to buy you a coffee and hear why and how you bought this location and got the main tenant."

THE PANDEMIC

Jerry may have thought he had seen it all in five decades, and the pandemic of 2020-2022 reminded him of a significant event some 40 years ago.

"Well, the pandemic really did not remind me of anything health-specific because we never had anything shut down business like that. I guess if there are similarities, it would be the tremendous tax changes, implications, and repercussions created by the Tax Reform Act of 1986."

The Tax Reform Act of 1986 turned the commercial real estate world upside down. Tax laws were changing, and the capital gains rate was going up. As a result, many of the tax benefits of buying commercial real estate evaporated. Jerry was quoted on the front page of the New York Times predicting that if the law passed, real estate values would "plummet by 15 percent."

He was wrong. Values dropped almost 30 percent. Suddenly CRE was a whole new game. Jerry said, "We didn't know if we could sell real estate without the generous tax benefits to investors. None of us really knew, so that's the only part of the pandemic that reminds me of something that happened previously."

I asked Jerry for advice he would share with folks looking to position themselves as authorities in the CRE brokerage space. For that answer, Jerry used an analogy based on his beloved Tesla.

"In today's market, finding out who owns electric cars is not difficult. We own three in our family. I'm on my second Tesla S. My son loves his Tesla. However, my wife still drives an S 550 Mercedes. Her Mercedes is a 2015 model. You would think a salesman from Mercedes would contact us to say, 'Jerry, it appears you're an electric car guy.

You won't believe the EV models that Mercedes Benz is coming out with.'"

Yet, I've heard nothing from a Mercedes salesperson even when I'm on service appointments and loudly complain about the cost of MB repair services compared to Tesla. My wife is a loyal Mercedes owner. We have owned numerous Mercedes models over the last four decades. You would think a salesperson would reach out to us. Nope, not even a postcard, email, or phone call."

Jerry's point? Does that take a lot of research? Does it take more digging than most commercial real estate agents are willing to do? Yes. Advisors who go the extra mile and do additional research will be better positioned as a valuable resource in the decision maker's eyes than simply a "real estate broker."

THE FUTURE OF BROKERAGE

What does Jerry imagine for the future of brokerage? He's seen everything and understands international brokerage offerings, national firms, networks, regional offices, and local independent boutiques.

"I don't see brokerage services going away. The users of commercial real estate, whether occupiers or investors, don't have the time to stay up on the marketplace, just like I don't have the time to stay in tune with what Mercedes is doing with electric vehicles or what another company may be doing. I simply do not have time for that."

Jerry believes your prospects and clients will continue to become better informed due to the internet and technology resources and therefore become better consumers. And when consumers understand the value, pricing, and how to access properties that are available online, brokerage fees will be compressed. Again, Jerry used an analogy to share his perspective.

"Just this morning, I was looking at some charges on my debit card, and there are a few charges from a physician. I thought about how I am not really receiving that much value from this physician in his 15-minute 'in & out' appointments. It's easy to look at it and ask, what did we do during my last appointment? Was it worth that out-of-pocket cost and my time? Clients will and should look at our value the same way."

And this should be one of the most important takeaways for you from reading this book. **Brokers Who DOMINATE can charge higher fees, and clients gladly pay because they understand the higher value they are receiving.**

Jerry is skeptical of the long-term viability of independent local boutique structures. He thinks the top 20 national firms will continue consolidating and gaining market share. As a result, they will win the most attractive assignments, even at the local level, while others will be competing for leftovers. Unless of course, you can offer a higher level of service and expertise than the national behemoths can.

And this view is supported by others as well. CEL & Associates, a leading commercial real estate strategy firm, noted in their May 2021 newsletter that "consolidation and retirements will reduce the number of real estate firms by 30-35%", and "up to 50% of today's brokers could be replaced by 'strategic advisors' who look more like a McKinsey or BCG Partner."

As for Jerry's specific future, that is still to be determined. But it's fair to say he doesn't need to work. "Beyond the financial reward, and don't get me wrong, the financial benefits of CRE are tremendous, but helping CRE investors recognize the opportunity or to eliminate a "pain" is the satisfaction. Wow, I never imagined it coming out of college, but I just hit 50 years in the CRE industry. That's a lot of experience to share!"

Jerry told me that ages 40 to 60, those 20 years, should be your maximum earning years. Everything else earlier, he considers "training and maturing." Fortunately for Jerry, his relationships and income are still going strong.

WHAT I LEARNED FROM JERRY

That is one of the many great lessons Jerry has taught me. Commercial real estate success is a long-term achievement requiring a long-term perspective. Unfortunately, too many brokers focus on the commission and the transaction versus the relationship. But in fact, it is the relationship that will pay you dividends, and some rather attractive ones, throughout your entire career.

Jerry Anderson remains, and forever will be, a broker who dominates, emphasizing **"Doing what is in the best interest of his client."**

Alas, it is time for the Mentor to move on to his next chapter. Yet, he will always be a mentor to me.

3 KEY TAKEAWAYS

❖ Brokers who DOMINATE bring more value. That puts them in a position to demand higher fees.

❖ Commercial real estate success is a long-term achievement requiring a long-term perspective. The relationship will pay you dividends, and some rather attractive ones, throughout your career.

❖ Commercial real estate users and investors will continually rely on Brokers Who DOMINATE, regardless of whether they align with an independent or national firm.

BOB KNAKAL
JLL, NEW YORK, NY

FAME AND FORTUNE

The dictionary defines fame as "the state of being known or talked about by many people, especially on account of notable achievements." Bob Knakal is the best-known broker in this book, famous to many in New York City and nationally. Oh, and he has made a heck of a lot of money as well.

I've lost count of how many people have told me they want to be "the Bob Knakal" of their local market. They don't understand what that means. Fame and fortune generally come to those willing to work their asses off every day. But unfortunately, a lot of that work is not glamorous.

Bob or "BK" as I have come to know him, was a kid from New Jersey who loved baseball and, even more so, baseball statistics. He attended the University of Pennsylvania, pitched on the varsity baseball team, and graduated from the prestigious Wharton School.

He found a job in commercial real estate by accident (you can learn more in my first book), and in November 1988, Bob and a colleague, Paul Massey, founded Massey Knakal. The firm consisted of Bob, Paul, and a secretary.

By December 2014, they had over 250 employees in four New York City offices and sold more buildings in NYC than any other company for 14 years in a row. In many of those years, they sold three or four times as many properties as the number two firm.

When I was planning my first book, dozens of people told me I must interview "Mr. Knakal". When I reached out to him, he asked what I did, and shortly afterward, he became a client. Yes, the best of the best are just that because they are committed to getting better. Bob was already successful and well-known but wanted to get even better.

Shortly after that, Bob would have the best year of his career. He shared that the "decision, getting coached by you, changed my life for the better, professionally and personally." It has enhanced my personal and professional life as well.

> *Regardless of where you are in your career, new to the business, or a master like Bob Knakal, we have programs to help you build the CRE business and life you have always desired. For more information, visit us at www.massimo-group.com*

On December 31st, 2014, after running Massey Knakal for 26 years and 46 days, Bob and Paul sold the company to Cushman and Wakefield for $100 million, and a new chapter in Bob's life began. That number may sound "life-changing" to most, but it was just another transaction for Bob, and he couldn't wait for his next deal.

Bob quickly learned that the benefits of aligning with a national company came at a cost. While the global reach and expanded capabilities are vital levers to creating greater business opportunities, bureaucratic policies can sometimes be frustrating if you're naturally more independent.

Eventually, Bob left Cushman and Wakefield and took 53 colleagues who had been with him since the Massey Knakal days to JLL. Today, Bob serves as the Chairman – NY Investment Sales at JLL.

Bob's team is like a small brokerage firm within a large national firm. Today, there are eight people on his team. They include an administrative assistant, a sales team manager, a public relations and media professional, two analysts, and three transactional associates.

The administrative assistant does a wide variety of things, from answering phones to scheduling meetings to paying Bob's bills and picking up his shirts from the cleaners. An administrative assistant should do anything to free up your schedule to spend more time on more important things. As Jack Daly wrote in his book *Hyper Sales Growth*, "If you don't have an admin, you are one."

Jon Hageman has been Bob's sales team manager and partner for 20 years. He keeps track of all the team's activities and assists with transactions. Jon's role has evolved over the years. He is now originating business opportunities regularly while continuing to manage the team.

The marketing team is responsible for maintaining the elevated level of Bob's presence campaign. You cannot be famous without having a robust presence.

A big part of Bob's fame comes from his grasp of the numbers and statistical analysis to illuminate market forces and trends. Clients, prospects, and other brokers have paid attention to his insight and observations for decades. So, when Bob writes an article, he knows there will be an audience. The marketing team's job is to make sure as many people as possible find out what Bob has to say.

They ensure Bob's article gets published and widely disseminated throughout social media. And Bob has recently committed to personally engaging in social media more than ever before. In addition, Bob records a video series, "The Knakal News Network", articulating the messages from the article. Public speaking and networking are also critical components of Bob's fame campaign. Because of the marketing effort, Bob can spend as much time as possible helping clients and creating new content.

Transactional associates are critically important in a middle-market investment sales broker's team. Any transaction progresses through several stages, and many things must get done. Tasks include preparing marketing blasts, gathering information for marketing materials, taking photos, conducting property inspection tours, researching and more. But a senior broker doesn't need to do all of them. Instead, they should spend time and energy on the crucial things only they can do. Prospecting is one of the essential things.

PROSPECTING

Does Bob personally prospect? Absolutely! Daily, in fact.

Bob believes prospecting is the most important thing a sales broker can do. I agree, yet an overwhelming majority of brokers do not implement a comprehensive prospecting plan. They get so busy with their deals that they do not set time aside for prospecting.

Bob blocks out time on his calendar two weeks in advance for prospecting. In addition, he sets aside at least 8 hours per week for prospecting calls. Like other successful brokers, Bob understands the value of telephone prospecting and keeps working to do it better.

Bob recently started a new prospecting approach. He identified his top 500 prospects and prioritized them from 1 to 500. Bob starts calling with #1 at the beginning of every two-month prospecting cycle and works his way down the list as far as he can go toward 500. If he makes it to 500 within two months, he returns to the top of the list. If he doesn't reach 500 by the end of the second month, he returns to #1.

This way, Bob ensures he hits his most important prospects at least six times every year. Many are not active in the market but own assets that Bob would like to sell. You can speak with an active prospect every week. But contacting someone who does not want to sell every two months is frequent enough.

This approach works for Bob because he has a team and because of the sheer size of the New York City market. You can implement a similar system, but instead of 500 top prospects, you will have 100. Then, when you have a team, you can concentrate on activities that will impact you and your team's bottom line the most. Prospecting is one of those crucial tasks.

BOB'S RESPONSE TO THE PANDEMIC

No market in the country was hit harder by the Pandemic than New York City. The city completely shut down during the summer of 2020. Sales volume during the pandemic was down 87% from the peak. With no transactions to do, Bob spent time significantly enhancing his primary research and market data.

A significant component of Bob's practice is land and development sales. Bob took the opportunity to drive and walk every single block in Manhattan south of 96th Street. It took Bob months to personally log every building under construction and every potential development site.

Many NYC brokers began to work on deals all over the US, where the sales volume was much more robust. However, Bob hunkered down in his local market and put himself in a better position to compete when the market returned. This work provided him with a lot of ammunition he is using today to win business and sell sites.

TECHNOLOGY AND THE FUTURE OF BROKERAGE

Bob begins thinking about technology and commercial real estate brokerage with some analysis of the current situation.

"If you think about the sales brokerage business, there are two main functions of the broker – 1) finding the buyer and 2) negotiating the deal. I believe technology can significantly disrupt the finding part of the function, but because buildings are not widgets, the human element will always be necessary."

Bob believes the effectiveness of technology will cause the brokerage business to transition to more of a consulting business. Consulting fees will replace brokerage commissions. Those fees will be much lower than traditional commissions. The transition may take 10 to 20 years, but it is inevitable. Are you ready for commissions to become "consulting fees?" What can you do to adapt sooner instead of later?

BOB'S LESSONS FROM THE LAST TEN YEARS

So, with some of the best and worst years in New York City investment sales, selling his company for $100 million and now working with two national firms, what are BK's top lessons from the last ten years?

1) "Having a great prospecting plan and setting aside time to implement it is essential. Prospecting is the gasoline that makes the car run. Without it, you are dead in the water. In addition, implementing a great plan allows you to dominate your market."

2) "Remember that you are your best client. No one will make more money for you over time than you will make for yourself.

Have the discipline to do the things you need to do. Take care of yourself – go to the gym, get proper sleep, and eat well."

3) "There is nothing more important than the big 3. Family, God, and Selling Buildings, in that order. Yes, selling buildings is that important to me. It allows me to have amazing experiences with my family. It allows me to spend time on my faith."

So, what's the secret to Bob's success and fame? Here are Bob's own words.

"I have always studied my local market and attempted to understand the market metrics better than anyone. Commercial brokers' most frequently asked question is, 'How is the market?' The overwhelming majority of market participants answer this question with adjectives such as "good," "slow," "hot," "we're busy," etc. However, answering with statistics demonstrates a deep understanding of how the market is performing. Clients want to work with brokers who have a great track record and understand the market fully."

What's next? BK is not done yet. Not even close. The kid from Jersey is still dreaming of baseball goals. But in this case, appropriately, it has to do with building sales.

"At the time of this writing, I have sold 2,257 properties in New York City over the course of my career, which began in 1984. My goal professionally is to get to 3,000. 3,000 hits has always been a monumental number for big leaguers in baseball. I would like to achieve that goal over the next 10 - 15 years.

My goals always revolve around getting better each year and helping those around me - clients and colleagues - to be their best. A big part of the satisfaction I get out of this business is watching those around me grow and excel."

3 KEY TAKEAWAYS

* ❖ Know your market better than anyone else. Clients want to work with brokers with a great track record and fully understand the market.

* ❖ Nothing is more important than having a great prospecting plan and setting aside the time to implement it.

* ❖ Remember that you are your best client. No one will make more money for you over time than you will make for yourself. Take care of yourself.

KYLE NAGY
PRESIDENT
COMMCAP ADVISORS
LAS VEGAS, RENO, AND BOISE

THE RESTLESS PURSUIT OF IMPROVEMENT

"Normal sucks". That's the title I used for Kyle Nagy's chapter in my Teams Built to DOMINATE book some 6 years ago. Kyle was creating a business, CommCap Advisors, that would purposely avoid the normal and focus instead on the exceptional. He had five team members then, today he has twelve. CommCap has expanded from its base in Las Vegas and has added offices in Reno and Boise.

CommCap Advisors is a full-service commercial mortgage banking firm. They specialize in the origination and servicing of commercial loans of $1 million or more. Kyle's team has closed over 800 loans, for an aggregated funding value exceeding $1.8 Billion.

That kind of volume demands leadership, which meant that something had to change. Over the past few years, Kyle's role evolved from player-coach into a coach more than a player. According to Kyle, applying Peter Drucker's observation that *what gets measured gets managed"* helped him make the transformation. Here's his description of how it went.

"After tracking my time for several months and measuring the effectiveness and joy of my weeks, I learned something shocking about myself. I enjoy focusing on CommCap as much or possibly more than doing deals. I was surprised, I am a self-proclaimed deal junkie."

"Deal dogs", as Kyle calls them, love working on deals. The next deal is the best deal. But if Kyle wanted CommCap to become exceptional, he had to stop counting deals and create a vision for the future of CommCap.

He also needed to create a vision of the "ideal client". First, Kyle and his team described their ideal client. They considered both psychological and demographic characteristics. Then, they changed their language and marketing to attract ideal clients. Kyle knows he can close loans with almost anyone. However, his hit ratio, enjoyment level and overall success are far greater when he works with ideal clients.

Brokers Who DOMINATE purposely structure their prospecting and marketing efforts to attract their ideal clients. They will not work with clients who don't meet their criteria. Sure, they may refer these clients to colleagues to keep a portion of the revenue, but if the client is not ideal, the broker and the broker's team will not engage personally.

Kyle and the CommCap team know they must keep the focus on their client's "ultimate goal." Here is how Kyle describes this key concept:

"I was introduced to a group several years ago through a broker. The borrower (we call our clients borrowers) owned several projects and was in the process of developing a long-term company strategy. Though a fee-earning loan opportunity was several years away, the borrower was transparent, curious about debt structures, and considered financing a vital part of the ownership equation. In short, they were my ideal client and considered me a part of the team.

"By defining their long-term investment goal and creating ideal future financing structures, they approached each project differently. When closing a loan three years later, the markets moved on us and the cost of debt increased substantially. With frustrations running high, we returned to the ultimate investment goal and moved from irritation to satisfaction. Without defining goals, we cannot measure success."

Kyle says most borrowers want the highest loan amount, best rate, best amortization, and cheapest closing cost. They want everything. But everything is not necessary to hit their ultimate goal, unless of course, they never set one. Brokers Who DOMINATE, including commercial mortgage brokers and commercial real estate brokers understand and focus on their client's ultimate goal.

As I noted earlier, CommCap has almost tripled in size since I last wrote about them. Kyle would tell you it took several years of discovery, success, and failure to understand who they are and why they exist. Once they articulated and documented those ideas, they infused them into CommCap's people and processes. Here is the outline:

"To clarify, we were busy closing loans, being successful, and making money without any great unifying, identity, or goal. We took a deep breath and asked ourselves, what is CommCap's differentiating characteristic? To figure out the answer, we spent hours at the conference room table having brutally honest conversations. In 2018, we came up with the answer and mission. By 2020, I realized our mission was really what we did, who we did it with, and not why we exist. We returned to the conference room after reading *Start with Why* and watching Simon Sinek's Ted Talk.

"Each employee was given a notecard and was asked to write down what drives them to get out of bed every day. Once they were done writing, I handed out a second card and asked, 'Why do you keep showing up at CommCap?' I collected the answers for the second card and read them aloud. I handed out another set and told them to try again, this time, taking 30 days to complete. We repeated it two more times and learned something about ourselves. The language we individually and collectively used to define our 'Why,' 'purpose,' or 'mission' consisted of common words.

"Relationship, growth, improvement, team, best, relentless, restless, leading, teaching, and learning. The emotional and physical enactment of those words is how we were already successful, how we hired, fired, grew, won, and lost. After wordsmithing them together in a meaningful way, we finally articulated what we already knew and believed. To all of us, CommCap is the Best Relationship Leverage for <u>Your</u> Growth."
It is these exact words "the best relationship leverage for your growth" that you will find on the company's homepage, on their website. As Kyle would tell me, individuals with similar beliefs succeeded, and those without left amicably. To attract the right people for the right roles, they intentionally incorporate the CommCap way into job postings and interviews.

ADAPTING TO THE PANDEMIC

Kyle believes technological advancements are reshaping the way we communicate and conduct business. The COVID pandemic introduced many of CommCap's older clients to new ways of receiving and sending information.

For the first time, CommCap hired a full-time Marketing Manager with a technology background. All social media platforms are leveraged to distribute content and brand messaging. They utilize phone messaging platforms to deliver 1,000 voicemail market updates within moments at minimal cost. They publish videos and blogs and are active on social media, including LinkedIn, Facebook, Instagram, and Twitter.

Kyle thinks the pandemic proved several things, most importantly, the character and value of people. Within 12 months of exiting the lockdown, they were working on a new vision or "Why" for the company. "It helped us to better understand ourselves, each other, and the company we have become. We invest in three things: People, Process, and Technology. The pandemic proved we have the right people and allowed us to better define who we are and the people we want to attract."

To ensure they are identifying and attracting the right people, CommCap outlines and explains their hiring, retention, promoting, and terminating processes during the interview process. Each position has an intentionally crafted job posting/description, scorecard, progression sheet, and uniform rating process. CommCap leverages the concepts of EOS (Entrepreneurial Operating System) and ghSmart (see the book *Who* by Geoff Smart and Randy Street) to create a predictable and enjoyable human resource experience for all team members. Based on their Glassdoor reviews, they're moving in the right direction.

THE FUTURE OF MORTGAGE BROKERAGE

Kyle believes the emergence of new technologies will increase CommCap's ability to reach potential clients. He also thinks artificial intelligence (AI) will play a big role in shaping the future, but that human beings will still be critical. Here are some details from Kyle.

"As with any other consulting-based industry, the growth of AI may replace a portion of our role. Perhaps, property level descriptions and financial modeling will be completed through AI in the near future. Any area with a defined set of inputs and desired outputs can be replaced by machine learning. Fortunately, relationships and customization of financing structures require a human touch. The science part can and will be replaced. The art of putting together a deal remains human."

THE TOP 3 LESSONS FROM THE LAST 10 YEARS.

"Beliefs drive behaviors. If you want to change any type of behavior, you must explore the underlying belief behind it. Without addressing your belief, behaviors will not change."

"Self-awareness is the single most important characteristic of being a good leader." The Notre Dame Athletic Director recently said. "Personally, I place a heavy degree of importance on self-awareness. If you're not honest with yourself, then you are, in essence, being dishonest with the people you interact with. You can't correct your shortcomings until you come to grips with your shortcomings."

"CEO Imposter Syndrome is a real thing and even the most successful, well-known, and loved CEOs struggle with it. You do not need to be perfect. Be authentic, have tough conversations, and let go of the outcomes."

TOP 3 LEVERS TO YOUR SUCCESS

"We invest in three things, People, Process, and Technology (PPT). First, we identify the right people by defining our core values and creating a recruiting and retention process to attract and retain them.

"We created process and structure to highlight team members' strengths, incorporate our unique differentiators, and simplify complex and convoluted steps.

We look at technology as an opportunity, not a cost. A new computer, software program, application, or CRM is not just a cost of doing business, it is an opportunity to innovate. By focusing on our People, Processes and Technology (PPT), we have almost tripled in size and have grown to three offices."

FUTURE GOALS

"The Restless Pursuit of Improvement." That's a sign that Kyle Nagy has in a prominent place on the wall of his office. He means more than his own improvement. He wants CommCap to be the best relationship leverage for everyone. "If I pursue improvement every day and offer everyone in and around CommCap the leverage they need to grow, no goal is large enough to describe what we can do."

3 KEY TAKEAWAYS

❖ Brokers Who DOMINATE purposely structure their prospecting and marketing efforts to attract their ideal clients. They will not work with clients who don't meet their criteria.

❖ Brokers Who DOMINATE understand and focus on their client's ultimate goal.

❖ Brokers Who DOMINATE focus on people, process, and technology, with an emphasis on the people who fit their culture.

Brent C Miller
SVN | Miller Commercial Real Estate
Executive Managing Director
Maryland, Delaware, Virginia, and
Pennsylvania

Family 2.0

Brent Miller, CCIM CPM, has always been a family man. He loves hanging out with his boys, his wife Amy and their golden retrievers. But, as I wrote in my 2016 book, Commercial Real Estate Teams Built to DOMINATE, he also loves overseeing his business family of brokers, property managers and staff. It's all family to Brent, and the location doesn't matter. It could be in the office, at the dog park, at the racetrack or anywhere else the team may be collaborating.

Since being profiled in that book, the SVN/Miller team continued to dominate their Salisbury, Maryland headquarters market in brokerage and property management. They also expanded to other like-size tertiary markets throughout a four-state region.

Brent transitioned from top producer to a player-coach to the broker in charge. Brent oversees the team's leadership, while his wife Amy handles finance and marketing. In addition, they invest in properties on the East Coast through their Synergy Investment Fund, a private equity real estate investment fund that focuses on distressed and value-add assets in emerging markets throughout the United States.

As I shared in my Teams book, a robust culture of cooperation and collaboration makes Brent's firm unique. That culture helps each team produce at a high level. In addition, collaboration between teams is easier because of the many strong relationships within the company.

Likewise, group production has grown, and they have invested in support staff. Several team members assumed new roles. Longtime Advisor and former Director of Property Management Rick Tilghman CCIM CPM became Managing Director and Sales Manager. He manages day-to-day operations. Brent continues to be the Broker of Record (MD, DE, VA, and PA) and mentors team members. Amber Bostwick is now Operations and Marketing Manager. Their leadership team consists of Brent, Amy, Rick and Amber.

Rick continues the traditions and best practices Brent established. He meets with all "Advisors" (a term used within the SVN framework) monthly to help them achieve their goals and objectives and strengthen their productivity and accountability to the team. Understanding all their team member's goals, not just financial ones, has always been a pillar of strength of the SVN/Miller approach. While most brokerage leaders focus on individual business goals, the SVN/Miller mantra is to fully understand every team member's personal, professional and financial goals. This understanding and regular monitoring help assure the individual and the team succeed together.

The brokerage team has changed several times over the years. At the time of the last book, they had just brought on two new, dynamic producers. From the start, they knew the new people were entrepreneurial in spirit and would one day move on. That took about four years.

There's a great lesson here for anyone who wishes to grow their brokerage firm. Strong-minded and individually focused brokers sometimes consume a disproportionate amount of time and attention. As a result, they are likely to move on when they think they spot greener pastures. Even worse, sometimes their competitive drive can extend to competing with teammates and poison the team atmosphere. Replacing them with more team-centric players can be a godsend for you, your team, your production and most importantly, the culture in your office.

CULTURE

Over the last ten years, Brent and Amy have found that a culture can be created top-down but that the team members, the relationships and the community keep it moving in the right direction. When they had producers focused only on their personal success, it negatively affected the positive culture they were attempting to maintain.

One way to increase the likelihood of a team member understanding and accepting your culture is to recruit new team members to CRE. SVN/Miller collaborates with Salisbury University's Mid-Atlantic Sales and Marketing Institute to assist with recruiting new brokers and employees through their internship program. In addition, leveraging your local community colleges, 4-year colleges, and master's programs is a great way to find the talent you can mold to your culture.

At SVN/Miller, teambuilding practices include annual picnics at Amy and Brent's house. In addition, there are pool parties, Christmas parties at the Miller's and retreats with team members at the Miller's vacation home in the Outer Banks. The SVN/Miller team also engages in team-building events such as laser tag, bowling, mud runs, happy hours, kickball leagues, charity golf tournaments and ropes courses.

Many firms will say they're "just like family". Most of the time, that's wishful thinking, but Brent Miller's team feels like a family in many important ways. Here's an example.

In the late 1980s, Henry Hanna recruited Brent to the firm he owned and became a mentor and trusted advisor to young Brent. After Brent and Amy set up their own firm, Henry came on board. Henry is much older than Brent or Amy. But, like many others in the firm, he often refers to them as "Mom and Dad".

TECHNOLOGY

The company has made several technological changes over the past decade. They moved from Loopnet to CREXi for their prospecting efforts, and from AppFolio to Buildout for their property and asset management services. Brent understands that technology is simply a platform. The people and processes allow SVN/Miller to win business, serve their clients and ultimately dominate their markets.

The team continues to cultivate a solid social media presence. They added a company YouTube channel, "SVN Advisor Insights". It provides an array of news and market updates, as well as landlord, user, tenant and investor advice from many of the SVN/Miller team members. The focus is not just on Brent or Amy, but on the entire team.

THE PANDEMIC

Brent and Amy have always worked hard to ensure their team and clients have the resources they need to succeed. So, it's no surprise they were equally proactive during the pandemic. As Brent shared with me:

"The day before the lockdown, we set all admin and support staff up with the ability to work from home. Most, if not all, Advisors were already able to do this. Because of this, we had no work stoppage due to a lack of access. However, things did shut down due to other factors.

"Since we also have an extensive property management and maintenance division, our office was deemed an 'essential business'. We opened back up after only a few weeks. During this time, we were flexible with work hours and initiated safety and sanitation protocols.

"Our Advisors were used to a weekly sales meeting each Tuesday morning. We continued that remotely with Zoom and later Google Meets. However, we felt that something needed to be done to keep our engagement up. So, during the first week of the lockdown, we started daily Zoom 'check-in' meetings with the Advisor and Property Management teams. Although the office opened back up quickly, some of the Advisors continued to work remotely, so the brokerage daily video calls continued for some time.

"We initiated and ran a weekly virtual meeting with the Mayor of Salisbury, community leaders/elected officials and the Greater Salisbury Committee with virtual updates to the community on how the COVID pandemic was affecting the business community. These weekly meetings continued for about the first year, then monthly for the next 6-7 months. In addition, we added a COVID Resources section to our website. Finally, we proactively assisted our clients (landlords and tenants) in obtaining assistance, including local funding, PPP programs, help with banking and lending institutions to enact deferred mortgage payments for landlords and subsequently deferred rent for tenants."

The results of this proactive approach produced yet another banner year for their team in 2021. That's impressive, but the benefits from SVN/Miller's actions set the stage for even greater success in the future. People who face a crisis together form strong, long-lasting bonds. Brent's firm earned a reputation for working with its clients, the local government and local businesses.

FUTURE OF BROKERAGE

Brent's vision of the broker of tomorrow is no different than the broker of today. In Brent's eyes, his team has always been "advising" more than brokering. Brent understands that facilitating a transaction is easy. However, an advisor's true value is putting their clients in a position to make a more educated decision on what's best for them. SVN/Miller defines this in their vision statement: *"Creating amazing value for our clients, colleagues, and community."*

THE TOP 3 LESSONS BRENT HAS LEARNED OVER THE LAST TEN YEARS:

"Diversify in asset classes in the brokerage and as a full-service CRE company to include full-service property management and maintenance. These areas support our CRE clients – creating deeper relationships and a chance for continued work together.

"Diversification also provides a stable income stream during downtimes, allowing us to keep the business running. For example, during the recession caused by the pandemic, we are proud to say that we were able to keep 100% of our staff and Advisors.

"CRE brokerage and management is a relationship business. Client relationships are key. You have to walk the walk and talk the talk. Character is always doing the right thing, especially when no one is looking. It comes back to you if you don't always exemplify positive and ethical character.

"**The importance of having a well-rounded company with an exceptional culture.** Consistency matters – especially in leadership. Many things are involved in this area. Examples include weekly sales meetings, quarterly community projects and the annual SVN/Miller Commercial Real Estate Forum. Not only do these things help to 'get things done,' but they also provide for a culture of stable leadership."

REGARDING SVN/MILLER'S SUPERPOWERS:

We usually talk about an individual's superpowers. Not this time. Brent listed the superpowers of *his firm* in response to my questionnaire. Here's what he thinks SVN/Miller does exceptionally well.

 A genuinely positive culture. Many say they have it; most do not. Brent and Amy constantly work to provide a caring and supportive culture. Those efforts pay off. "One of our employees asked a few weeks ago – which of your sons is going to come in and take over the company when you retire because I never want to work anywhere else but here."

Branding and adhering to the SVN Core Covenants. "We strive for this and live it. We have had Advisors, employees, and staff members who thought they did, but in reality, they did not. Because of this, they didn't fit in and have since moved on their own accord or at our request. The key here is that the other team members have created this dynamic, more so than us."

Community service / Giving back to the community. SVN/Miller supports Habitat for Humanity, Chesapeake Housing Mission, SVN Dog Park and gift packages for military servicemembers.

As for the future, Brent's vision is simple. Continue to grow their brokerage and property management business and CRE Investment

Fund. And when he says "their", he isn't only talking about him and Amy, but the entire SVN/Miller team, their extended family. Family 2.0.

3 KEY TAKEAWAYS

- ❖ Facilitating a transaction is easy. However, a broker's true value is putting their clients in a position to make a more educated decision on what's best for them.

- ❖ Strong-minded and individually focused brokers consume a disproportionate amount of time and attention. Replacing them with more team-centric players can prove to be a godsend for you, your team, your production and most importantly, the culture in your office.

- ❖ Technology is simply a platform. It is the people and the processes that allow you to win business, serve your clients and ultimately, dominate your market.

James Nelson
Avison Young
Principal and Head of Tri-State
Investment Sales
New York, New York

Habits

I wrote about James Nelson in my second book, "Teams Built to DOMINATE." Then, James was the wonder kid from Connecticut who was taking the New York market by storm.

Smart, savvy and committed to the craft of commercial real estate brokerage, Nelson was involved in more than $100 million worth of business in his first two years of investment sales. The New York Real Estate Board (REBNY) named him "Most Promising Rookie Salesperson of the Year." That was just the start.

Since then, James has continued his climb to become one of the dominant brokers in the New York City market. Ten years ago, he was a partner at Massey Knakal. Yes, the same Bob Knakal whose story I shared earlier in this book.

"We had an incredible run which culminated with the sale of our company to Cushman & Wakefield, one of the oldest and most respected real estate brands in the world. This was the ultimate compliment that our unique business model, culture and hard work had paid off."

As I shared earlier, Massey Knakal sold for $100 million. Paul Massey and Bob Knakal were very generous to their partners. James says:

"This sale was an incredible thing for me, personally and professionally. At the beginning of 2015, the transition to Cushman & Wakefield could not have been easier. My sales team kept our offices, and C&W told us to keep selling and see if we could assist our clients in other ways. We now had a truly full-service global platform to leverage."

In 2015, James' team of twelve people was handling upwards of 40 sales a year, making him the company's number one capital markets salesperson in the US. James then expanded his team to include a dedicated mortgage broker and retail leasing team member. This is a common approach for Brokers Who DOMINATE. They understand the opportunities for leverage and growth by expanding to other verticals. They remain specialists, but they offer ancillary services to address their current clients' growing needs and the developing needs of the marketplace.

MOVING TO AVISON YOUNG AND BUILDING OUT THE TEAM

After three years at Cushman, James was ready for his next challenge. "I wanted to take my team approach, which had previously operated amongst multiple brokerage teams on the floor and bring it to a company where we could cover all of New York City together. That new company was Avison Young. I am grateful to the Massimo Group and others for helping me write an extensive business plan. This approach would involve first analyzing the marketplace and the competitive landscape." You're welcome, James.

James takes great pride in building out one unified sales team. He has strong views on what a great team should look like.

"I believe the key to success for my team has been to create a unified front. Most brokerage firms or agents compete with each other internally for business. My team philosophy has always been that if one person wins, everybody wins. To truly accomplish this, compensation has to mirror culture. Therefore, my team shared and continues to share commissions on every transaction."

His goal is to be the most active boutique sales team for the upper-middle markets. That means $10 – 250 million. James wants his team to offer their clients the best marketplace opportunities. The team must vet opportunities and not take overpriced properties from non-motivated sellers. That only spins everyone's wheels.

"Our team is proud to have secured as high as a 13% market share in Manhattan in this price range. That might not sound like much, but in a big city, that represents a lot of sales. Our 5-year plan is to close 100 sales for $25 million in revenue. We are well on our way."

13% market share in NYC! Let that sink in. What would be the impact on your career and life if you were to achieve a 13% market share in a highly valued opportunity?

GOALS AND PLANS AND HABITS

A key for James is to support his goals with action plans and the action plans with the right habits. James is a big fan of James Clear's book *Atomic Habits*. To achieve a goal, you must define what the goal is. Then you must create a plan to achieve that goal. So far, so good. Now develop habits that define daily what you must do to work that plan. James refers to those habits as "systems".

"We must put the right systems in place to achieve these goals. I am incredibly proud not just of the sales team we have assembled, but the dedicated operations team that allows us to do this business."

By now, you should get the sense that James is a continual learner, voracious reader and consumer of information. That is another "atomic habit" of Brokers Who DOMINATE. What about you? What information do you consume? Is it the latest Amazon Prime series or endless hours of SportsCenter, or is it information that will impact your career, your life and your legacy? The good news is that since you are reading this book, you are taking a small step toward becoming a Broker Who DOMINATES.

Since moving to Avison Young, James has focused on creating more valuable content. During the pandemic, James began interviewing his clients and friends when market velocity came to a standstill in New York City. That led to his podcast "*The Insiders Edge to Real Estate Investing - Game-Changing Strategies to Outperform The Market*", which now has had over 250,000 downloads. James also shares this information through his social media channels, including LinkedIn and Instagram.

James is currently working on two books. You can find his content on jamesnelson.com. When you go to the site, you will notice James doesn't talk about how great he is, or his incredibly impressive bio. Instead, he focuses on helping people gain the inside edge in real estate investing.

During the pandemic, James attempted to launch a real estate investment fund on a crowdfunding platform. While he won't say it didn't work, the opportunity to buy at distressed prices came and went very quickly. "I couldn't pull this together in time, but at least I gave it a shot. There are still great opportunities to invest in the market, so I'm not giving up on this." I'm sure James learned a lot that he'll be able to use further down the road.

Another common habit of Brokers Who DOMINATE is practicing what they preach. James is a top sales broker in arguably the most dynamic market in the world. And he also personally invests, helps others invest and advises investment funds and firms.

In fact, last year when Brad Ahrens, who is also profiled in this book, contacted me about creating a new coaching program for commercial real estate brokers looking to syndicate their own deals, I jumped at the opportunity. Today, CRE Investor Coach helps CRE brokers accelerate their pathway to becoming a principal and yes, James serves on our Board of Advisors.

The Future of Brokerage

When I asked James how he imagined the future of brokerage, he told me about Malcolm Gladwell's speech at an Avison Young event. Gladwell spoke about how to best position yourself in a rapidly changing world with technology and the influx of data.

James said Gladwell believes there is almost too much data out there today. He used the tragic events of 9/11 as an example. Gladwell noted that we didn't foresee the event because we didn't have the data. Quite the opposite, there were plenty of warning signs, but we were inundated with information. As a result, no one could connect the dots or make a clear decision on how to use that information. James thinks commercial real estate is in a similar situation.

"There is so much information out there. You could say an investor doesn't need a broker. They could look up listings on Loopnet or research property owner information directly on Reonomy and cold call the owner. But would they know what to look for? I believe the job of the broker won't ever be replaced. The technology and data will make their jobs easier, but it is most important to know how to make this information actionable."

JAMES'S TOP 3 LESSONS LEARNED OVER THE LAST TEN YEARS

Never stop learning. "What I love most about this business is that I learn new things daily. I am constantly looking to improve my team and my knowledge. I am a voracious content consumer, whether it's daily newsletters on the market, reading books from inspiring leaders or podcasts on self-improvement."

Create the proper habits. "This is a literal page out of James Clear's book, but having the right habits day in and day out is what creates success. I'm not saying that goals aren't important, but this last decade has taught me that business is not impervious to market conditions. When COVID hit, I didn't start sleeping until noon and binge on Netflix series. I kept my same daily work habits even though I didn't see the immediate results."

Have a coach. "During the middle of my career, I thought I had figured everything out. My business was growing. I thought, why do I need to invest the time and money for counsel when things are going so well? The answer is that I ended up on the transaction treadmill that Rod speaks about. If you don't have a coach and mentors pushing you out of your comfort zone, you can't make quantum leaps in your business and life."

JAMES'S SUPERPOWERS

"I always put myself in my client's shoes – I am always thinking of how I can achieve success for them first and foremost.

"I am constantly looking to improve my personal and team business. As mentioned above, I am always learning ways to do things better.

"I have the best presence in the NYC marketplace. I deliver the highest quality content that helps investors make the best decisions."

As for the future, "I would like to be known as the go-to source for real estate investment advice. If you look at my website, I offer the inside edge to real estate investing. I see myself in 10 years having multiple best-selling books with a global network of top investors. They will come to me for advice on when to make important investment decisions.

By then my brokerage team will be a well-run machine. I will be able to continue to source business but, have a strong execution team that can run sales from start to finish, affording me time to run a real estate fund that will make investments. In addition, I will have the flexibility to work from wherever I am so I can spend more time with my family and friends."

I am sure James will continue to be disciplined and install habits to achieve these and all his future goals.

3 KEY TAKEAWAYS

❖ Understand the opportunities for leverage and growth by expanding to other verticals. You should remain a specialist but offer ancillary services to address your current clients' growing needs and the developing needs of the marketplace.

❖ Practice what you preach. You cannot truly be an investment specialist unless you invest in a property yourself. Likewise, you cannot truly understand the mindset of a tenant unless you are a tenant yourself or a business owner unless you own a business.

❖ Your habits are the action steps that reinforce your discipline to achieve greatness. Your habits define what you must do every day to achieve your goals.

JILL DUEMELAND
DUEMELANDS COMMERCIAL INC.
CEO AND PRESIDENT
BISMARCK, NORTH DAKOTA

THE 3 SECRETS

Jill Duemeland is the personification of "work smarter, not harder". Over the last fourteen years, she's been in the office an average of three days per week. She's never once been in the office five days in a row.

Jill was one of the "Young Guns" in Brokers Who DOMINATE. As I wrote then, her real estate roots go back to 1905 when her great-grandfather, George, moved to Bismarck, North Dakota and sold land to settlers as they got off the train from the east.

Jill was early in her career then and busy raising a 3-year-old, with another baby on the way. For her, back then and now, it comes down to focus and efficiency. In 2012, Jill shared her benchmarks for her highly effective and efficient early success. She called them eating frogs, power working, always working to bring value and focusing on the deals with a high probability of closing. She decided to seek clients who met three criteria:

· There was a high probability the first deal will close.
· There was the possibility for multiple deals.
· The client was one the firm could serve well.

Using those criteria, Jill would select clients who would do a lot of repeat business. Going after repeat business is a high-leverage activity, so it naturally made Jill and her firm more effective and efficient. Jill built on the successful legacy of her family business, all while raising her four children, now 14, 10, 8 and 6.

While being in the office 3 days a week, Jill has amassed a very impressive client list. Retailers include Caribou Coffee, Costco, Mattress Firm, Chipotle and Crisp & Green. There are REITs such as Centerspace (CSR), Sterling Real Estate Trust and Dakota REIT. Jill has also represented several development companies and owners such as Oppidan in Excelsior, MN, Granite Peak Development in Casper, WY and Visconsi Companies in Cleveland, OH.

That might be enough for many brokers, but Jill continued to grow and evolve and develop her unique way of doing business. Recently, Jill wrote to me that she was ready to share three additional secrets to making more while working less. My eyes widened when I read that. "Making more by working less'" is one of the driving principles of the Massimo Groups' coaching programs. It's the reason many of our clients engage us in the first place. So, I was eager to learn Jill's "secrets".

"Making more" is important but not to run up numbers in a bank account like a video game score. "Making more" allows you to gain margin in your life for the things that matter most. That's why we help our clients build growing and scalable businesses without neglecting other important things.

My eyes got even bigger when I realized how Jill used the time she spent out of the office. Check out her family travel schedule:

- January – US Figure Skating Sectionals in Michigan and Travel Hockey every weekend

- February – US Figure Skating Nationals in Colorado and Travel Hockey every weekend
- March – 5-day Big Sky Montana Ski Trip (off the grid and not checking email)
- April – 11-day Hawaii Trip (off the grid and not checking email)
- May and June – 2-week family camp trip (off the grid and not checking email) We have taken family camping road trips from North Dakota to California, Pacific Northwest, Maine, and the Smokey Mountains.
- June – weekend at the lake working remotely Fridays.
- July – working remotely from the lake.
- August – working remotely from the lake September – in office
- October – 5-day Hilton Head Trip (mostly off the grid) November – in office
- December – start travel for skating and hockey

Jill's three criteria for client selection laid the foundation for profitable brokerage. They concentrate marketing on high-leverage activities. The three secrets she developed since Brokers Who DOMINATE describe how you can run a profitable brokerage to gain maximum margin.

For Jill, that begins with relationships.

SECRET #1 – RELATIONSHIPS

Jill thinks all brokers should develop a close team. Her close team includes two important people.

She calls the first one "a partner in crime". Your partner in crime is your foxhole person. You split all commissions 50/50. You cover for each other when you are on vacation or sick. Jill says that's the only way you will ever have a phone-free vacation.

Jill and her partner-in-crime brainstorm together on the best way to navigate a deal. They proofread each other's letters of intent and purchase agreements. They cover each other's blind sides.

The second key person is an administrative assistant. Jill uses the popular personal assessment instrument DiSC to guide her hiring. Most commercial real estate brokers are good at influencing, persuasion and are good with people. They score as D or i on the DiSC instrument.

Jill wants someone who is a C on the DiSC instrument as an administrative assistant. According to DiSC, they "tend to place the emphasis on quality, accuracy, expertise and competency". Jill says they will pay attention to the details that you might miss. They will complete the tasks that are critical for your business but will be last on your to-do list. Here's how Jill describes the benefits.

"A typical scenario is I am at a hockey rink; I can connect with a client on the phone regarding a property, my assistant can prepare the letter of intent or purchase agreement draft and I can be watching my son's game."

Jill points out that you should not "go with your gut" when hiring. Plenty of research supports her position. Most of us are simply bad at making wise hiring decisions without following a thorough process and using an assessment tool.

Jill uses the DiSC assessment and as I detailed in my book, Teams Built to Dominate, we use the AVA platform. This tool allows us, and our clients, to make better people decisions and provides a roadmap for ideal individual and team communication.

If you are interested in learning more about how you can assess your current team's natural behaviors of that of a recruit for your team, please visit www.creperform.com

Once you have a partner-in-crime, Jill strongly suggests the two of you "Go on Tour". Jill and her partner-in-crime will set up a series of meetings with prospects on a single day. Jill's firm covers the entire state of North Dakota so they often "Go on Tour" to neighboring markets.

Jill and her partner-in-crime went on a series of tours in the months just before COVID. Those visits paid off big time. Let Jill describe what happened.

"The relationship building of those face-to-face meetings was priceless. Especially when March 20, 2020 hit and every tenant in our restaurant portfolio said they were not paying rent. Our conversations about coming up with a plan were easier given our relationship and recent conversations."

Face-to-face meetings are powerful. As Jill says, "In our new world of Zoom and Microsoft Teams, the face-to-face meeting is getting lost, but I guarantee you will always learn more from a face-to-face meeting than over the internet." She's right. Lots of research highlights the fact that in-person communication is more nuanced and more likely to build trust than voice alone or even voice with video, such as Zoom.

SECRET #2 – PROCESSES

Most brokers do not have documented processes that they follow in every aspect of a transaction. That's one reason Jill thinks that having well-documented processes and following them is a competitive advantage. She didn't always think that way.

When she was starting out, she and her father clashed over whether Jill should spend time writing processes and procedures. Jill's father, George "Skip" Duemeland, thought it was a good idea. Jill thought there were better uses of her time, like calling prospects. She also thought processes should be long and formal and were a pain to write. Here's how that changed.

"I had a wise mentor that said to me, 'Just write down WHAT you are doing, WHILE you do it. You, my friend, have just created a process.' That simple phrase was a game changer for me because I did just that. Now I have a process for everything and a framework for my administrative staff to follow and new agents joining our team."

In addition to the process, having templates for every part of the transaction helps save time. A common phrase in Jill's office is "Trust the Process". When they follow the process, they see the results.

SECRET #3 - DATA

Jill and her team record and track every piece of data they can. They record every new contact, their cell phone number and all pertinent information. They record every comparable they can get their hands on. Many brokers have a CRM, but the value of the platform is only as high as the amount of data entered into it.

Jill believes that most brokers are poor at data entry and can only do 2 clicks before moving on, so they're not likely to enter all the data she wants. But remember how she used a psychological instrument to hire. Her administrative assistant is a C, meaning the assistant values both quality and accuracy—the perfect person to enter every bit of data correctly.

Comprehensive, complete, and accurate data are part of Jill's firm's competitive advantage. As she says, "Clients seek us for data and advice, but it is only good if we have it."

WHAT'S NEXT

Jill shared that she would continue to follow the habits of 10 years ago that she outlined in the original Brokers Who DOMINATE. Pairing those original habits with the three secrets outlined above will ensure that Jill will continue to be a Broker Who Dominates for as long as she desires.

3 KEY TAKEAWAYS

❖ Identify your own partner-in-crime. He or she will be a person who can cover for you when are on vacation or sick. This is the only way you will ever have a phone-free vacation.

❖ Create Processes. Write down what you are doing while you do it. Now you have a process.

❖ Develop your own habits of success. Some great books I have read on building powerful habits include *Eat That Frog*, *Atomic Habits* and *The 4 Disciplines of Execution*

BO BARRON

THE MARINE BECOMES "THE MAN"

When I first wrote about Bo in 2012, I titled his chapter "The Marine". Bo was a 3rd generation commercial real estate whiz kid. Smart, but not driven. In fact, you could say he was unfocused and unmotivated.

Then, one night when he was draped over his college dorm room couch, he saw a commercial that would change his life. It was a recruiting ad for the Marines. He'd probably seen it hundreds of times, but it caught his attention this time. So, he went to see a Marine recruiter. When Bo asked what the Marines would offer him, the recruiter said, "I wonder if you have the metal to be in my Marine Corps."

Bo accepted that challenge. He went to boot camp and language school and served as a cryptologic warfare linguist. He absorbed the Marines' excellence culture and worked hard for the first time in his life. He even completed his college degree. When he left the Marines, he was both smart and driven.

Bo returned to his hometown of Owensboro, Kentucky ("God's Country," as Bo would tell you) to work at his dad's local real estate firm. However, Bo had a bigger vision for himself and the family business. He earned his CCIM and secured a franchise with Sperry Van Ness (now SVN). This change would prove to be the first of two times Bo would build a dominant commercial real estate company in his family's market.

Since then, Bo has helped run SVN as their VP of Organization Development. He had a high impact run with me and the Massimo Group as COO and became a CCIM instructor and a CRE investor. He was also the COO of a food safety tech start-up.

Now, Bo is back expanding on his family legacy. After he bought the firm from his father in 2020, he rebranded it as the Barron Commercial Group. When he reflects on his journey, Bo says this.

"At every stop along the way, I picked up experiences of leadership styles, different business models and experiences in different roles. All of it, the good and the bad, helped me develop who I am as a leader and has shown me how to grow a world-class company full of people I'm blessed to lead and work with."

Bo understands that leading a brokerage team does not include competing with its members.

At the Barron Commercial Group, Bo plays the role of CEO and rainmaker. As Bo describes it,

"My greatest value to the company is providing opportunities while coming alongside my team to make them successful. My role as a leader is to benefit those I lead. The more successful I can help them become, the more successful the company will be and the more successful I will be."

BARRON COMMERCIAL GROUP

Barron Commercial Group has a solid mission statement. Based on the ideas in Donald Miller's book, *Building A Story Brand: Clarify Your Message So Customers Will Listen.* I love it.

-o0o-

The Barron Commercial Group Mission

Many businesses and investors find it hard to navigate the rough terrain of a commercial real estate transaction. As a result, businesses can become caged in space that hinders their profitability, and investors can leave money on the table.

We study our markets and connect with influencers so that we can put businesses in spaces where they can thrive and advise investors on how to maximize their opportunities.

Barron Commercial Group exists because if commercial real estate is optimized, more businesses and investors will experience success.

-o0o-

The core of his firm is Bo's brokerage team. It consists of Bo, a junior and a senior producer, a property/transaction manager and a virtual assistant.

His junior assists in marketing and some analysis and works on all Bo's transactions.

Bo's junior and the senior producer work on the opportunities they generate through their prospecting. Bo's prospecting is mainly for their benefit. Ideally, half of their income comes from their prospecting, and the other fifty percent comes from leads due to the company's presence and from Bo's prospecting.

Bo's admin does many routine tasks so Bo can concentrate on higher-leverage tasks. But Bo's assistant is different from many admin assistants. For example, Bob Knakal (who you have already read about) has his admin complete tasks like picking up Bob's shirts from the cleaners and running errands. Bo's admin can't do that because Bo's admin is virtual.

He used a firm that provides virtual assistants to businesses. Bo pays them as a vendor, so he has no HR/compliance worries. He can add hours or tasks as his needs change.

Bo and his team leverage Buildout, Crexi and Loopnet and uses Realnex as their CRM. They log every listing into STDB.com and use the database feature to build a list of potential buyers or tenants. Bo understands the best brokers proactively market their listings by targeting prospects and making calls. He wants his team to make calls, connect and help people realize their opportunities and solve their problems.

Strong brokerages look for ways to increase their revenue streams. One stream for Barron Commercial Group is self-storage. Bo's father and grandfather were homebuilders. When interest rates spiked around 1981, people quit buying houses. That left Bo's dad with crews he wanted to keep busy. The answer was self-storage.

It's a good business because the $/square foot for rent compared to the cost of building is about as good as you can get in CRE. It's also recession-resistant and throws off a lot of cash.

Bo's self-storage team consists of two full-time employees who work with a contracted management company. Bo brought on professional management a year ago for two reasons. One, he thought great third-party management would more than pay for itself. Two, Bo has expanded BCG's self-storage investment geography. As a result, BCG can now buy or develop in any market and turn it over to the pros.

Bo spends 50% of his time exploring investment opportunities and building his syndication. On this investment side, you see Bo's CCIM background and passion for numbers. Here's how he describes what he does.

"On the syndication side, I'm identifying dynamic markets with significant job growth – especially in basic employment. This is because basic employment has a multiplier effect that significantly increases total employment. So, when you can predict total employment growth, you can apply the market's PER (population to employment ratio) and predict population growth. Then I can quantify, for example, how much more self-storage a market will need – or how many more apartment units – or office square footage, etc.

"If I can find a great site in one of these dynamically growing markets, I know I can develop self-storage (or another property type) that will lease up and stabilize quickly. This will in return, provide growing cash flow for the investment group while significantly increasing the property's value."

As I said, Bo is now "The Man" in his market and beyond. The Marine became The Man.

RESPONDING TO THE PANDEMIC

Bo's team didn't need to adapt much to the pandemic. It was much easier to get people's attention when things slowed down. Bo's team doubled down on prospecting and proactive marketing campaigns and had their best year ever. Great lesson here. When things slow down, most of your competition starts running scared. It's the best time to increase your efforts, particularly in prospecting and marketing.

Bo also worked on his operations' efficiency and effectiveness. They evaluate all their systems and processes to find where they can improve. Bo outlines one key area.

"My focus is on growing the company by adding great sales talent. We're a small company with three producers, including myself, and we're looking to add another producer. My small market is mainly an owner/user market, and our bread and butter are $300k - $500k leases and sales transactions."

THE FUTURE

Bo thinks the proliferation of transparent information will weed out brokerage hobbyists. Buyers, sellers, landlords and tenants benefit from the information commercial real estate professionals provide. In Bo's mind, the more information that is out there, the fewer agents are needed. "Those bottom-tier agents who just parrot information that is readily available aren't going to make it."

Bo believes the brokers who will make it and continue to thrive will be those who position themselves this way:

- They simplify the process of transacting by making things easier for their clients.
- They analyze data and predict demand to assist their clients in making great decisions in markets and situations that lack clarity.
- They focus on their client's goals obsessively.

BO'S TOP THREE LESSONS FROM THE LAST 10 YEARS

Bo's top 3 lessons from the last ten years are focused on good old-fashioned values that reflect his Owensboro, Kentucky upbringing.

Success depends on the grunt work. It isn't about technology or the rise or fall of the market. It is about the blocking and tackling of brokerage. Bo admits he has geeked out over social media and internet marketing, but he knows none of that does any good if he is not on the phone talking to owners and prospects or if he is not building a network of influencers and connectors.

Teamwork is key. The team is more effective than the sum of its parts. Bo's team comprises professionals with different strengths. Bo's role as the leader is to define their roles, clarify expectations and put them in a position to use their strengths. Then he trains, coaches and supports.

Family is more important than business. Bo acknowledges there was a time when he worked too much. "Even to the point where my wife asked me if I loved her. I was crushed. I did love her – still do (she rocks!) – but I wasn't acting like it. I'd come home for dinner, help with the kids, and then go back to the office multiple times a week. I was gone too much, and she was neglected. I'm embarrassed looking back. Nothing is more important to me than being a great husband and father. With my team, I work less, am present more with my family, and the business continues to grow."

So, what does Bo believe are his three greatest strengths? Let him tell you himself.

"**My network** – I'm the third generation in our business, and I benefit from the man my father is, and my grandfather was. In our market, I have opportunities because of the men they are/were. I have inherited so many relationships from them.

"**Leadership** – Beyond teeing up opportunities for my team, I coach and train. The more successful they are, the more the company grows. Therefore, I should be answering these two questions continually – 'What do you expect from me?' and 'How am I doing?'

"**Always learning** – I don't think I've had an original thought in my life, but there is little I enjoy more than learning. I read at least one book weekly, and I'm striving to learn from others' successes and failures. These lessons I pass on to my team, and we implement them into our business."

Bo, however, is far from the tail end of his career. In his mid-40's, he is just beginning to leverage all the strengths he noted above. Over the next ten years, he has goals for himself, his family and his team.

Professionally, Bo wants to grow his company, so they have a team full of world-class people who love what they do and benefit greatly from being a part of the company. Bo is convinced that Barron Commercial exists to serve his team. He wants his team to be wildly successful.

Today, you would never picture Bo as being unfocused, undriven or unmotivated. On the contrary, today Bo is "The Man" in his business, community and family. He just happens to be building a world-class boutique brokerage firm and investment practice along the way.

The Marine became The Man.

3 KEY TAKEAWAYS

- ❖ The best time to increase your efforts, particularly prospecting and marketing, is when most of your competition is running scared.

- ❖ Focus on efficiency and effectiveness. Evaluate all your systems and processes to identify where you can improve.

- ❖ Expand your revenue channels – such as creating syndications or investing in CRE.

The Coppola-Cheney Group
Lee and Associates
Phoenix, Arizona
Transparency, Systems, and Velocity

Including the Coppola-Cheney Group (C2) in my second book, Teams Built to Dominate, was a no-brainer. This team is among the most dominant teams in the CRE brokerage industry.

Lee & Associates has been in business for more than forty years. They have more than 65 offices and over 1,000 brokers. Craig Coppola is the firm's top-performing broker, not just this year but in the entire history of the firm.

Craig and Andrew Cheney are two of only 33 people in the world who hold the three most coveted designations in the industry: CCIM, CRE and SIOR. Mr. Coppola has 3+ decades of experience and specializes in representing landlords and tenants in the leasing and selling of office properties. He has been the top producer at Lee & Associates 24 times. He was a finalist for the NAIOP Office Broker of the year 25 times and won the award six times.

Craig has completed over 80 marathons and ultramarathons and is a world champion in Taekwondo. In addition, he has authored five books. This book is my fourth book. I've only completed one triathlon and avoid all physical conflicts, except on the lacrosse field.

You and I could spend our time comparing ourselves to top performers like Craig. But as Theodore Roosevelt said, "Comparison is the thief of joy." So instead of comparing yourself to the dominators in this book, put your time and energy into learning from them.

Craig's partner, Andrew Cheney, dominates in his own right. He is a former professional tennis player and remains a competitive athlete. Andrew evolved from team runner/junior broker to partner to lead originator. He has completed over 1,200 transactions totaling over $1 billion—someone else to learn from.

Over the last decade, the Coppola-Cheney team has matured, and roles have become much more defined based on individual strengths, interests and priorities.

Craig has transitioned away from many of the day-to-day responsibilities. Instead, he participates in key transactions and has assumed the roles of advisor and trainer. These days he focuses on relationships, shaping team culture, and mentoring team members.

Andrew Cheney has become increasingly responsible for bringing in new business. He has also focused his attention on becoming a stronger leader in both the community and at Lee & Associates.

Gregg Kafka was an associate when I wrote my team's book. He's now a Principal and Partner of The Coppola-Cheney team. He is the team's resident deal slayer, closing on average 50 transactions each year. Gregg concentrates on growing existing client relationships and has recently begun taking on more new-business generation.

Nick Whitehouse is the newest partner on the team. He started as a runner in 2020 and became a partner focusing on tenant advisory in 2023.

Craig and Andrew have added new team members to fill needs such as database administration, graphic design and more, as well as bringing on several runners. According to Craig, the most crucial member of their team has been Chelsea Clifton, who started as an assistant over a decade ago and is now Director of Operations.

Chelsea has brought consistency and organization to the team, creating processes that yield consistently excellent results. Under her leadership, the team defined the unique abilities of each team member and put them to use in their individual spheres of genius.

The team systematized their prospecting processes. By introducing a team-wide cold calling competition, they have not only increased the number of leads generated but also shared the responsibility among all team members. Here's how Craig describes what they did.

"We created a giant scorecard of our team's prospecting activities and results. Since most brokers are competitive by nature, we have found that by turning cold calling into a competition to see who can get the most calls, conversations and leads, we are able to generate far greater business development."

I LOVE THIS! Nothing is more honest than transparency. Transparency to your partners, and transparency to yourself. If you want to have a full pipeline in the second quarter of the year, hold a prospecting competition in the first quarter. If you want a full pipeline all the time, then compete all the time.

The team also refined their blog, known as *The C2 Voice*, to make it more helpful for their 30,000+ readers across the nation. A recent innovation is a video blog. It's called *"Ten on One"* to indicate that each edition spends ten minutes on one issue. By sharing industry news and think pieces, they've established themselves as thought leaders and authorities in commercial real estate.

STREAMLINING PROCESSES

"We've also spent a lot of time implementing tracking systems that are personalized to our team to better measure our results and outcomes," says Craig Coppola. Their transactions are much more automated since they started using CRE OneSource, a commercial real estate technology company.

Craig believes the tools offered through CRE OneSource (www.creonesource.com) have completely streamlined the day-to-day tasks of each transaction. He was so impressed he bought the company in June 2021. He says, "The software has made a huge difference in how we run transactions, track our time and maintain organization. We use it as a service to add transparency to our clients. It also brings us way more insight into our business."

Craig is not only using this platform for his own benefit. He has made this tool available to others, including competitors, providing a new revenue stream.

Think about what tools you use, the ones you feel give you a competitive advantage. Did you ever think of purchasing them or becoming an exclusive licensee? At Massimo, we did something similar to Craig and became the exclusive licensee of the AVA Natural Behavior platform for the commercial real estate industry. This tool helps us and our coaching clients make better personal and team decisions.

The lesson here is to think beyond your commissions. Think about expanding your services and your revenue channels. Dominators don't simply live by the transaction.

The Pandemic

While most tenant representation businesses took a severe hit during the pandemic, the Coppola - Cheney Group expanded. How was that possible?

"Our robust, existing client relationships allowed us to actually grow our business during the pandemic, to sell/lease a few other product types, like land and industrial. What really worked best for our team was focusing on small and medium transactions. Holding out for larger tenants didn't work, as the market for those larger tenants was and still is very competitive with the national firms."

Again, dominators find opportunities and solutions for their clients and themselves.

Another vital component to dominating as a broker is to create "experiences" for your clients. Creating experiences is something we preach with our coaching clients at the Massimo Group. Craig and his team are not our clients, but their strategy has shifted to helping their clients make the office experience as memorable as possible when designing common areas and tenant improvements. As companies return to the office, their strategy has revolved around counseling landlords on navigating this return as effectively as possible.

THE FUTURE OF BROKERAGE

Many brokers are concerned about the potential reduction in brokers as technology evolves and industry consolidation continues. Craig isn't. His team is positioned for continued success and growth. Looking back at the last ten years, he can quickly identify his three greatest lessons, and not surprisingly, they all are focused on his team,

"First, a broker has a very defined ceiling of complexity without a team. The talents, unique abilities and support system that a team provides will take an individual much further than they could get on their own.

"Second, having different skill sets and ages on the team adds valuable diversity. As the markets change and technology evolves, it's crucial to have these different perspectives contributing to the team's success.

"Finally, you must spend time training and developing your team to make it succeed. Those who do not invest in the personal growth of their team members will see their overall team success suffer."

C2's SUPERPOWERS

Craig shared these thoughts about the team's superpowers and what makes them one of the most dominant in the industry. He labels them "levers".

"Confidence earned by building a great team. By putting in the time and effort to assemble a strong team, we can move with greater confidence, trusting in our collective abilities.

"We are striving to be great every day. On our team, we use the word 'kaizen', meaning continuous improvement.

"We care for our clients more than our competition. Client relationships remain at the heart of everything we do. Without these relationships, we would not be where we are today."

Craig thinks **Velocity** is the key thing that makes his team stand out from the competition. I asked him to explain what that meant.

"No one moves like we do. Our team is nimble and current. Not only do we stay up to date with the market, but when each team member is functioning in their unique ability, we're able to execute faster than anyone else in the industry. We are constantly in the market, participating in deals and events. We understand the market better than anyone else and communicate that knowledge with each other and with our clients.

"Our velocity of work relies on everyone in our team knowing and living in their Unique Ability — the zone of genius, where passion and talent meet. Velocity loves to move from Unique Ability too, and in turn, deals run on velocity. When our deals are fueled by velocity, we are more productive, which keeps our clients happy and coming back to us again and again."

You may not be familiar with the term "Unique Ability." Dan Sullivan defines it this way: "Your Unique Ability is you at your best. It's the hard-wired set of natural talents that you're passionate about making use of in every area of your life." For example, if you're managing a team, the idea is to build on a team member's unique abilities, so members do what they're good at.

It's no surprise that Coppola-Cheney strives to be the top office brokerage team in Arizona every single year. They want to continue establishing The Coppola-Cheney Group as a legacy brand within Lee & Associates and the national CRE market. They have specific revenue goals every year. Finally, they want to train all their brokers to be successful. That means spending time with them and mentoring them.

"Personally, all members of the team are working to build wealth as we reach financial independence. This applies to everyone, from the brokers down to the runners and the rest of our team. We also encourage everyone on the team to have a healthy and prosperous home life. Every team member sets personal goals that we believe are just as important as professional goals.

"Overall, the goal over the next ten years is to build up The Coppola-Cheney team to continue excelling in the industry. Most brokers retire, and their business disappears. We are building this team to be generational."

As Craig retires, Andrew will take the leadership role. They have built their team to continue and grow. Team members' experience, market knowledge, and effective processes will contribute to a successful team in the future.

3 Key Takeaways

❖ Think beyond your commissions. Think about expanding your services and your revenue channels. Dominators don't simply live by the transaction.

❖ Nothing is more honest than transparency. Transparency to your partners, transparency to yourself. Transparency creates healthy competition, which in turn creates exponential growth.

❖ When your deals are fueled by velocity, you are more productive, which keeps your clients happy and coming back to you again and again.

Mark Myers
Managing Director, Walker & Dunlop
Chicago, IL

Still the Expert and Getting Better

What an incredible ten years it's been for Mark and his team! When he appeared in the original Brokers Who DOMINATE, Mark had already made an impression on his peers and clients. Shortly after that book was published, Mark was inducted into the Midwest Real Estate Hall of Fame. That was just the start.

Mark specializes in senior housing properties of all types including assisted living facilities, independent living facilities, freestanding memory care facilities, skilled nursing facilities, continuing care retirement communities and age-restricted apartments. This seems like a great niche today, but it wasn't necessarily a slam-dunk specialty ten years ago.

When Mark left Marcus and Millichap for Walker & Dunlop, his first task was to fortify his team to serve his expanding client base best. He and his primary partner, Josh Jandris, have created an industry-leading team.

Mark and Josh recently took on a third full partner, Brett Gardner. Brett was a senior executive with Direct Supply. That company provides procurement, building management, construction and other services to Skilled Nursing Facilities (SNFs) and senior housing. Brett knows virtually every executive in the industry and leverages these relationships to provide tremendous value.

They also grew their analytical team by adding two experienced underwriters for senior housing and long-term care transactions and three business development professionals. After the pandemic, Mark's team continued to expand, adding Gideon Orion, an expert in seniors housing and long-term care advisory. Clients want to work with brokers with inventory, and Gideon has begun filling the team pipeline with sellable properties.

A key lesson here is that Mark continues to grow his team to serve his clients rather than himself. Yes, growing for the sake of earning more personal margin is a sound tactic. However, ultimately you grow to either expand your services to existing clients or expand your reach to new verticals.

That development is paying off. The team is busier than ever, and their average transaction size has also increased geometrically.

How do they do it? Mark says they start with adept underwriting and pricing. They create terrific marketing presentation documents that display the facts and the story. The story describes why certain assets are underperforming and how the Buyer can realistically improve operations to create significantly more cash flow. The materials and every contact are designed to demonstrate the team's expertise.

Mark outlined the benefits of being an expert in his 2012 profile. As Mark shared back then, "If you're the expert, you're the one the clients are likely to trust." Here is a small sample of Mark's expertise. Imagine that you're a prospect listening to Mark's analysis.

"There are crossover buyers from other real estate product types, such as multi-family investors, and other

investment platforms, including private equity. In fact,
for some periods during the past ten years, private equity
outpaced REITs in transaction volume in senior
housing. This is a surprising feat since REITs have
historically represented about 2/3 of the total
acquisition volume in our space. Private equity is
attracted to the business component of seniors housing."

Brokers Who DOMINATE know their market and the players and control the inventory and all the resources their clients seek. The changes Mark and Josh made to the team have allowed them to take a more institutional approach to their advisory. This includes generating complex modeling, world-class marketing material, targeted buyer concentration for each transaction and effective client-facing and communication tools. Here are three examples of how Mark and Josh have become "better experts" in the last ten years.

TECHNOLOGY

A data vault has streamlined operations during the past ten years. Rather than a flurry of emails requesting data, each bidder signs a confidentiality agreement and is granted access to a password-protected data vault. The vault contains the due diligence and marketing materials for a given offering. The vault may also contain the Seller's form Letter of Intent (LOI) and Purchase and Sale Agreement (PSA) along with an Operations Transfer Agreement (OTA). The PSA spells out the real estate deal terms, while the OTA outlines the operational terms associated with the Old Operator transferring responsibility and licenses to the New Operator.

Minimum Bid Strategy

But technology is not the only enhancement. In the last ten years, it is the Minimum Bid strategy the team has applied that has been enormously effective. Let's have Mark tell us about it.

> "With the Minimum Bid, we have turned the bidding and negotiation process on its ear, putting the Seller more in control. The bidders are now asking, 'How much higher than the Minimum Bid do I need to bid to be competitive?' The sky's the limit on price. This, combined with the fact that more bidders join the bidding process when the Minimum Bid is set sufficiently low, only helps garner a higher price.

> "This is highly counterintuitive to traditional real estate thinking. The old rule was to ask for the highest possible price because you can always come down but not go up. Well, with a Minimum Bid, you can only go up, and there is no ceiling on price, only a floor. An added benefit of the Minimum is that no bidder can submit a stupid-low or "value" offer, which some buyers find a preferred tactic if there is no Minimum Bid."

The proof of this strategy is in the pudding. Mark's team regularly exceeds the Seller's pricing expectations.

The Expert and the Pandemic

During the pandemic, Mark knew that for most of his clients, it was not wise for them to sell properties, given the industry's uncertainty. So, Mark's team took the approach of not forcing the hand of their clients to sell. Instead, they provided them with research and connections to locate PPE (Personal Protective Equipment) and other infectious disease control items. They spread the word about methods for keeping residents connected with their families and physicians, despite being in lockdown due to COVID. They helped explain to clients what other providers were doing to retain and protect residents and staff and helped them find ways to address cash flow issues. They became "frenemies" with competitors.

Their strategy of being a trustworthy advisor benefited them in the long run, as the effects of the pandemic waned in 2021 and transaction volume exploded. The long-term advisory approach seems simple, yet it is elusive for most brokers.

What's Next for Brokerage?

Mark recognizes that standard brokering will become a commodity. His response is simple.

> "We will continue evolving into advisors rather than traditional salespeople. The pandemic only made it more important to advise clients on what's truly best for them, whether it's the timing of a sale, repositioning for sale or not selling at all. Sometimes, refinancing is better than a sale, as this may provide tax-deferred cash to the Seller. Other times, it's better to reduce third-party contract staffing, increase monthly rates,

implement ancillary services or wait until prepayment penalties on debt have expired before considering a sale."

When you ask Mark about his continued success, he focuses on the same elements he shared in 2012. As I wrote then, "he believes we can accomplish almost anything we set our minds on. All it takes is finding the role models, coaches and mentors who can show us the way, plus a lot of hard work."

Mark feels just as strongly now. He quickly thanked Walker & Dunlop's Chairman and CEO, Willy Walker. "I cannot say enough about Willy Walker and his Executive Team at W&D. Willy is a world-renowned executive who has created more shareholder value than just about any company aside from Amazon."

MARK'S LESSONS FROM THE LAST TEN YEARS

Regarding the top 3 lessons from the last ten years, Mark relies on lessons from some of the sport's greatest athletes. He says, "I have taken lessons from GOATs (Greatest of All-Time) in their respective sports, such as Tom Brady, Tiger Woods or LeBron James." Mark says they do three things differently and better than other players.

"They constantly try and improve." Tiger Woods revamped his entire swing. Brady changed teams, as did Lebron, a few times. Brady perfected the slant pass to get rid of the ball more quickly, continue moving down the field and promote energy on his team.

"They thoroughly enjoy the game and play for their love of it." These all-time greats would hold out or sit out if it was all about the money. No, they love what they do; are grateful and feel privileged to suit up each day. It's the same for Mark. Mark loves what he does and cannot imagine doing anything else.

The third lesson is a bit different. Mark has observed that not all the GOATs are happy people. Some are miserable, never having enough, and always seeking the thrill of the next thing. That leads to a powerful insight.

"All the victories in the world don't make you who you are nor give you true eternal joy and fulfillment." Mark says, "That comes from a relationship with the One above and with fellow human beings, particularly one's family and friends. I'm learning (not there yet) to make the main thing **the** main thing."

And as far as a few key strengths that Mark feels help differentiate him and his team, Mark is not bashful in stating that what sets him apart is the people around him. Mark strongly feels that he has "the best parents, best wife, best professional coaches and mentors, partners, team, company and the best clients".

Secondly, Mark is humble. As Mark shares, "It requires humility to realize you are not God's gift to mankind. You must learn much and discipline yourself daily to accomplish a great goal. It takes the same humility to look to others, including teachers, mentors, partners, spouses, writers, speakers and more, to improve. And humility is needed to spend the time and effort to keep improving yourself rather than become lazy and give in and give up."

Mark credits his wife for much of his success. "My wife is the one who told me, 35 years ago, that I should look at those who are successful in whatever it is I wish to succeed, find out what made them successful and emulate them."

It seems so simple, but how many people humbly admit they don't currently have the skill set, education or environment in which to succeed and seek to change those dynamics to catalyze success?

3 Key Takeaways

- ❖ Grow your services to existing clients or expand your reach to new verticals.

- ❖ Sell smart. Become adept at underwriting and pricing. Create terrific marketing and presentation documents that tell a story.

- ❖ Emulate the most successful, the GOATs, get mentors, get a coach and be a lifelong learner.

Matt McGregor
Colliers International
Executive Vice President
Seattle, WA

Matt McGregor and Bill Condon were the competitors who became partners I wrote about in Teams Built to Dominate. Matt and Bill were both leading industrial brokers in the Seattle market, where they competed directly for many years. Their shared values and mutual respect drew them together. Bill said, "In my mind, he was the only guy in the market I could partner up with because we were aligned on personal goals and business perspective."

For this book, I focused my update on Matt McGregor as our paths have crossed several times over the years while, unfortunately, I have never had the honor of personally meeting Bill. Matt and Bill still compete in many ways. Whether running triathlons, coaching youth sports or pursuing advanced degrees in their craft, they are seemingly racing each other to perfection.

The Last Ten Years

The past ten years have been very rewarding for Matt and Bill. Their business has increased five-fold and they have had four years of record-breaking production. They have successfully up-leveled their pursuit capabilities, landing five major household brands as long-term national tenant clients. They also have completed several $100 million plus investment deals with more in their pipeline.

Matt helped shape the direction of Colliers' nationwide industrial real estate platform. He is also one of the 10 founding members of Collier's exclusive Tenant Advisory Team, an invitation-only group comprising

10 of the company's most successful tenant brokers. This team's objectives are to study the tenant representation business on behalf of Colliers and determine what resources they need to build a competitive, global tenant representation platform.

Matt is a Colliers' Industrial Advisory Board member and a founding member and board member of the organization's Logistics and Supply Chain Management practice group. In 2021, Matt and Bill completed master's degrees in supply chain management at Michigan State University, the country's top supply chain management program, according to U. S. News and World Report.

LEVERAGING TECHNOLOGY

Ten years ago, Matt said their team was "a leader in technology". He didn't mean that they had the newest, spiffiest tech tools. The true test of whether a team is a technology leader is whether they get a competitive advantage from how they use technology. That's the kind of "leadership" Matt and Bill have continued. Here's a partial list of the technology tools the team uses.

- ZoomInfo: profile companies and individuals
- Vidyard: Enhanced emails with video content
- StoryMaps: Presentation software to explain market dynamics
- Asana: Project management software for sequencing pursuits and organizing transactions
- Wiser: Site selection software
- Apto: Data based with a Salesforce engine
- Team Podcast: Used to share original content and industry dialogue
- Ceros: Interactive digital presentations
- Intuiface: Digital presentations

Matt and Bill have a podcast, *"Industrial Advisors"*. The primary audience is brokers from competing firms. Since the podcast was launched in 2016, its audience has grown substantially; it's now a top-rated podcast in several countries.

ADDING PEOPLE

You can't grow without adding people. Matt and Bill beefed up their business development team by adding two prospecting-focused associates to support their local landlord representation and national tenant representation business.

Technology is a powerful lever, but without support, technology is just added expense and frustration. Matt and Bill have added several pieces to their team over the last decade. They designed every change to help them provide a more innovative, analytical and technology-based service offering for their clients.

They added an "Innovation Specialist" to help run all their technology-based marketing and account management. She handles the production of the podcast.

To enhance their market presence, they have a team of creative marketing folks who work on all custom pursuits. The team comprises three individuals specializing in speaker development, electronic marketing, art, digital marketing and presentation software.

As of the writing of this book, they are in the process of hiring a Business Development Manager. Who will coordinate all pursuits, podcast guests and general marketing related to business development.

Supply Chain Analytics

Matt shared that the most significant change they implemented in the past ten years has been their focus on supply chain analytics. They have worked to hone their ability to sell this service to occupiers, as they believe it is a true value-add for their prospect's business and is something not offered by other brokers. They worked with Colliers' new Supply Chain Solutions group to develop a tool that leverages supply chain analytics to help with site selection.

The Supply Chain Solutions group includes members focusing on solutions for Opex reduction and service improvement. Workforce analytics specialists help clients leverage data about their businesses to make informed real estate decisions. Consultants provide insights on supply chain network optimization, site selection, process analysis and warehouse layout development.

This was a collaborative development with Colliers' technology team, the Occupier Services group and three of Colliers' key brokers. It assists brokers with macro analysis for site selection.

Fourteen critical datapoints help clients analyze real estate as a cog in their supply chain, allowing them to evaluate real estate from a total cost perspective. This is a powerful benefit because real estate costs only account for +/- 6% of the actual cost of the location.

Consider site selection, for example. Site selection affects transportation costs: "Transportation consistently ranks as the number one cost driver in overall distribution cost, frequently more than 50% of those costs." In fact, 94% of the spending includes supply chain analytics assessing inbound and outbound freight, delivery costs, warehouse design labor, utilities and other criteria for total cost analysis.

STREAMLINED PROSPECTING

Bill and Matt have leveraged technology to streamline their pursuits. In this case, they use Asana project management software to manage a sequential 7-step process that boosts efficiency and means the team can always know where a given prospect is in the pursuit process.

Their Sequential 7-Step Prospecting Pursuit Process starts with a pre-call to assure that the prospect meets the criteria for pursuit. Then the team uses a top-to-bottom approach. They cold call the highest-level person that would touch real estate, then work their way down. Here's how the process works.

- The first follow-up is a Vidyard email with a promised delivery.
- The second follow-up is a coffee mug mailer with a team brochure and a personalized letter.
- The third step is a strategy document personalized to one of the prospect's assets/leases.
- The fourth step is a Draw Shop video delivery assuming the client's portfolio justifies the approach.
- The fifth step is a 10-minute webinar explaining our competitive differences.
- The sixth step is a handwritten thank you card for taking the time to view our materials and competitive differences. They include an article or other value-added information specific to the prospect's interests.
- A live pop-in visit allows for a brief but formal introduction.

Not everything is technology dependent. Matt and Bill have found value in using industry associations to develop and maintain connections with prospective clients. They both make it a point to be active in these types of organizations and to serve on the board or in another leadership role where possible.

The Pandemic

Everyone in CRE had to act quickly to respond to the pandemic and adapt to how they approached their business. Bill and Matt's team was no exception.

Matt says the most significant and most successful change they made was accelerating the incorporation of supply chain management analytics into their business. Matt and Bill were about halfway through their supply chain master's program when the pandemic hit. The plan was to finish their degrees and build an analytical tool in the next five years.

When the pandemic turned the "supply chain" into a worldwide dinner table conversation topic, they knew they'd need to move faster. They were awarded their degrees in 2021. They began developing an analytical tool to help clients and set the team apart. They also started the hiring process for a supply chain-focused team within Colliers.

Matt and Bill value face-to-face interactions and sending prospects tangible items. The pandemic made that almost impossible. Here's how Matt describes the situation.

"When the pandemic sent everyone to work from home, those tools were no longer effective because face-to-face meetings were discouraged, and many people were reluctant to provide their home addresses for mailings."

In response, Matt and Bill adopted tools to help them create digital, interactive materials that could provide an engaging experience for the people who received them. They now leverage tools like Storymap and Ceros for interactive digital presentations. They have found these work well when in-person delivery is not an option and even help them enhance face-to-face presentations.

The Evolution of Brokerage

Matt believes that clients are becoming savvier in understanding basic real estate considerations. They can increasingly locate space and negotiate contracts on their own. He thinks what will set brokers apart will be the ability to leverage technology and analytics to demonstrate how various spaces can provide clients with cost savings. Matt believes we'll see brokers take a more consultative approach based on a more in-depth understanding of their client's business. We'll see them invest heavily in specialized technology and tools.

Top 3 Lessons from the Last Ten Years

I asked Matt the top three lessons he had learned over the past ten years. Here's his answer.

"Continuously learn. When I started in this business, and even to a certain extent today, many aspects of it were, for lack of a better word, archaic. I've found that those who find sustained success invest in themselves and their business and make it a point to go beyond basic brokerage to stay abreast of technology and how it can add value for clients.

"Stay about 12 months ahead of the curve. I do my best to read enough and analyze enough data to advise my clients on what's coming, not just how to react to what's already happened. This has served me well. We started noticing how supply chain issues could significantly impact clients' costs well before the pandemic hit, which led us to further our knowledge in that area and helped us set ourselves apart as the pandemic went on.

"Be fun and easy to do business with; seek out clients that are the same. This one is almost self-explanatory, but being enjoyable to work with and knowing how to mix work and play helps create strong relationships that prove to be fruitful in the long term."

MATT'S TOP 3 SUCCESS LEVERS

So, what are three success levers that make Matt successful? Matt says they are:

"I have an innate drive to be number 1, and because of that drive, I'm able to assess my strengths and weaknesses to identify where I can improve and understand what I can use as differentiators.

"I am not afraid to invest in education, even well into my career. Many people would have balked at the idea of going back to school to get a master's degree at 50 years old, but I believed that it would help me create a competitive edge, which it most certainly has. I believe so strongly in this kind of investment that I make it a point each year to identify one big area that I would like to gain more knowledge in or improve at and then take measurable steps to make that happen by working with a coach, taking a class, etc.

"I've built a business model around having fun. Enjoying what I do and whom I work with has played a big role in my sustained success."

THE NEXT 10 YEARS

"I set a goal each year to be physically stronger than I was the year before. So, I'm always working to be able to do more push-ups and other strength exercises. In 10 years, I should be able to do quite a few!

"Professionally, I'm excited to see how Bill's and my incorporation of supply chain management into our business continues to evolve. It's already helped us to grow our business significantly, and we've only just begun. I expect us to have a full roster of national tenant clients who rely on our supply chain analytics to assess their real estate needs and for Colliers to have grown their Supply Chain Management group into an even bigger powerhouse."

3 KEY TAKEAWAYS

❖ Stay about 12 months ahead of the curve. Read industry and non-industry trends and analyze enough data for your clients on what's coming, not just how to react to what's already happened.

❖ Build out your team to serve the market's needs.

❖ Innovate your marketing and present yourself differently than your competition.

Ken Ashley
Cushman & Wakefield
Executive Director
Atlanta, GA

The Servant

What do you want to be known for? Many brokers want to be known as top producers or recognized for their deal-making ability. Ken Ashley and his team, whom I wrote about in my second book, Teams Built to DOMINATE, want that too. But Ken would prefer to be known for his contributions to the industry and community. So, instead of listing his top-producer awards and industry honors, let's review some of Ken's contributions.

Ken is Executive Director at Cushman & Wakefield. Formerly, he was Chair of their Tenant Advisory Group, comprised of the company's highest-performing brokers. He is an award-winning instructor in his trade organization, CoreNet Global.

Ken completed the prestigious Leadership Atlanta program. His "civic rent", as he calls it, includes serving several not-for-profit organizations. Some of the positions Ken holds include Board of Directors, Atlanta Area Council of Boy Scouts, Board Chairman, Fulton County Sheriff's Foundation, and Board Member, Crimestoppers. He also serves on the Board of African American Real Estate Professionals and as Vice Chair of Spirit of Atlanta Drum and Bugle Corps.

If this civic rent was not impressive enough, in his "free time," Ken also founded the #CREi list and #CREiSummit. There are lists for Twitter, LinkedIn, and Instagram. As Ken shares, this is where "CRE industry leaders share their secrets on how they build their digital relationships, social media following, and information on how to create a stronger personal brand and close more deals."

As I outlined in Teams Built to DOMINATE, Ken was an early adopter of social media. Now he's contributing to the industry by helping other brokers use social media more effectively.

"I love to see people succeed, and I love positivity. The CREi: Top Influencers in Commercial Real Estate lists highlight genuinely good people doing amazing things in our world. These lists are intended to lift those who are great contributors, leaders and influencers in our industry."

KEN ASHLEY'S PIVOT MODEL

Over the years, Ken has kept his core team small, with just three people. He uses what he calls a "pivot" model. His team works with other colleagues in the office on specific accounts and client assignments. Clients get great service and attention. Ken's team can concentrate on finding and maintaining quality relationships with high-potential clients. Everybody wins. Ken explains how it works.

"I know what I'm good at; I love to work on deals and expand/establish new account relationships. I don't wish to be a corporate manager of a large team of people. Fortunately, we have an amazing, talented pool of tenant reps in my office, many of whom work independently. When I kick up a new transaction in Atlanta, I can literally walk down the hall and ask one of our skilled tenant reps to help.

"I love this 'pivot' model where I can hire someone I like, trust and respect to work on the new deal. Likewise, after 27 years at Cushman

& Wakefield, I've developed a network of brokers around the Americas' and even around the world that I work with again and again. I believe in hiring the right expert on a project-by-project basis. This approach keeps us nimble, and I believe it's the best way to serve our clients and run the business."

Ken's team tracks strategic relationships in an A, B, and C format. As Ken shared with me,

"Stephen Covey talked about 'putting the big rocks in first'. If you spend all your time chasing any deal (little rocks), you will potentially run out of time to chase the deals that propel you forward. Just being 'busy' is not necessarily an indication of future success or a profitable business.

"We have created an X-ray process that helps us evaluate opportunities. We want to first put the big rocks in - the most potentially profitable and interesting business to pursue. There are many, many types of deals we do not want or need to work on. We know where we excel, and that's where we shine our light."

Of course, they strongly emphasize social media presence and presence marketing. Marketing and sales are different. Sales is speaking with the intent to convince. Marketing is about influencing what your targets think about you before you walk into the room.

Nine times out of ten, prospects will take your call if you can establish a reputation as an expert in a market or subject. Ken uses social media, traditional media, public speaking and writing articles to establish an expert presence.

The Pandemic

When the pandemic hit, Ken ramped up his thought leadership efforts. He wrote for Forbes to share his knowledge with others. And he increased personal engagement with those in and outside his industry. Ken's writing demonstrated his expertise on topics in commercial real estate. Like the other Dominators, what worked for Ken and his team during the pandemic was prioritizing relationships with clients. Taking a long-term, low-pressure approach to making decisions was a winning strategy.

Ken can also tell you what didn't work during the pandemic. "We had many misguided companies make decisions out of FUD – fear, uncertainty and doubt. They opted for very short-term leases with no tenant improvement allowance and gave landlords the flexibility to reset rates in the near term. Even worse, some decided to talk to their landlords directly without guidance (or landlords began these talks on their own). Overall, the pandemic disrupted normal and prudent decision-making as black swan events often seem to do."

The pandemic also allowed Ken to emphasize the value of focusing on talent and people when developing a real estate solution. Ken sees talent as the reason for the sticks and bricks. He says, "Don't lead with the office tower, but instead those workers that will occupy and use the built environment they're given. One real estate director in my organization once said, 'we need to meet employees where they are'"

The Next 10 years for CRE

Ken understands the transition the commercial real estate industry is going through. He firmly believes that market knowledge and transaction process expertise are the price of admission and give you a seat in the arena. But he thinks those who are going to be on stage and win fight after fight must pay attention to three things.

First, brokers who prioritize focus on the client's business imperative will succeed. They will speak "executive", which means they understand a client's business and its challenges. They will assist their client in navigating through "CLMs" (Career Limiting Moves) and then help them focus on successfully executing increasingly complex challenges. Real estate is only a tool to help solve a problem. You will be a resource for your clients when you know landlords, market conditions, rates and lease contract fundamentals. Real estate is most companies' second highest cost after labor.

Second, brokers must prevent their clients from chasing "shiny red balls" of technology. You will need to be responsible for selecting "proptech" that will help transactions and real estate operations, not hinder them. These tools can supercharge mundane processes and may save big money. But the wrong tool can be frustrating, expensive, and highly distracting. Even if you aren't 'the' expert, you must find those at their company or network who can track and advise on tech tools.

Third, brokers must make the complex simple, like explaining acronyms and the why to the what. There is a deep process and tradition in many real estate verticals. Brokers can help "crosswalk" real estate lingo and help the client understand why they should care. You must be prepared to show your homework in terms of analysis and justifying your reasoning. As a general rule, it's best to present an executive summary. Think and talk as if your words will be presented to a Board of Directors that wants "just the facts" and not the 9th level of detail.

Top 3 Lessons from the Last Ten Years

"Don't underestimate the power of habits and rituals. Motivation is an emotion, and emotions come and go. Habits tend to get acted on no matter how you feel. In fact, if you get *out of* ritual or habit, then you feel bad. Setting the proper business habits can be jet fuel for your career.

"Time. Is. The. Most. Valuable. Thing. Determine your vital few tasks, the 20 percent of what you do that generates 80 percent of your results. Calculate the value of your time so you know what tasks you can assign to others.

"A strong sense of personal responsibility is a crucial characteristic of almost all successful people - certainly those who make their living in a commission-only environment.

"As commercial brokers, we wake up unemployed every morning and have to have the self-discipline to do the right things for our business every day - day after day. When people see brokers 'winning' by executing a very large transaction, they don't see the incredible focus to complete the many steps necessary to identify, pursue and win the business. And most times, no one is standing around with a whistle on their neck and a bullhorn in his hand coaching you up. Success is ultimately up to the individual to execute over a long time - certainly at the senior levels in this field. You need fire. in. the. belly every AM!"

Levers to his Success

I asked Ken to describe his success levers. Here's what he said.

"Strong emotional IQ. Practice 'tactical listening,' which is a verb. Study nonverbals. There is a HUGE amount of information being generated by the other person or people in any setting. Get the focus off what you are going to say next in a conversation and instead listen and read what those around you are saying.

"Be a servant leader. In other words, the military leader eats last. I take personal responsibility for things and own my mistakes.

"What sets me apart is that I always stay curious. This includes staying on top of trends, constantly studying, teaching classes, writing articles and sharing my findings with clients."

It's no surprise that Ken's focus is on continuing to find more businesses to serve. "I'm a capitalist and believe growing my portfolio of work is a noble goal." In addition, he has goals to write a book for people trying to enter our industry. Ken firmly believes we are responsible for reaching back down the ladder, just like others did for him.

3 KEY TAKEAWAYS

- ❖ There is a false belief that spending time away from transactions is counterproductive to your career. Nothing could be further from the truth. Invest that time in building relationships.

- ❖ Focus on the big "rocks" first. If you spend all your time chasing any deal (little rocks), you will run out of time to pursue the deals that propel you forward. Being "busy" is not necessarily an indication of future success or a profitable business.

❖ Assist your client in navigating through "CLMs" (Career Limiting Moves) and help them focus on successfully executing increasingly complex challenges.

Brad Umansky
Progressive Real Estate Partners
President
Inland Empire, California

Head Coach

Back in 2012, when I first wrote about Brad, I shared his fascinating journey to CRE success. Brad learned he liked to work independently by working on a horse farm. He tried the hotel business and discovered it was not for him.

He went to Israel for four months and lived in a kibbutz. A kibbutz is a socialist community. Laboring in this community, Brad realized how much he loved capitalism. More so, he realized he wanted to be self-employed, which led him to a fifteen-year brokerage career before starting his own firm.

In 2012, Brad was a couple of years into the growth of Progressive Real Estate Partners (PREP), a boutique brokerage firm specializing in brokering retail properties in Southern California's Inland Empire region. They specialize in landlord representation, investment sales, land sales, tenant representation, gas station and car wash sales.

Today, Brad is a great team leader who calls himself the firm's head coach. The firm has grown to fifteen real estate professionals and has consistently been a leader in this marketplace. Progressive Real Estate Partners has completed more retail lease and sale transactions than any other regional brokerage firm over the past decade. That's impressive, but Brad has an additional perspective:

"Although the number of retail lease and sale transactions within our geography is one measure of our leadership. Our active involvement in industry associations, our contributions of market information to the industry and continuously marketing ourselves as the Inland Empire Retail Experts has led to many recognizing us for our contributions to the retail market within our region."

STANDARDS AND VALUES

A pivotal element to Progressive's success is maintaining its standards and values. For Brad success at PREP starts with a broker being a good person.

"One of the great benefits of leading a firm is you get to choose who works with you, and I have no tolerance for working with people whose values do not align with mine. As a result, our team members are hardworking, honest, team-oriented and family-oriented individuals. Helping good people achieve their goals is highly motivating to me."

Think back to the Coppola – Cheney chapter earlier in this book. Their team was established on standards and values as well. Their values are different than PREP's, but they are as important. What standards and values does your team have and live by?

Yet there is no doubt that production is a significant measure of success. Brad states that clearly.

"Progressive Real Estate Partners is a business and not a charity. Part-timers or people that are in a declining stage of their career are not for our team. The cost to operate a brokerage firm is far higher than most people think, and there is too much financial risk to support people that are not doing their best to achieve. Furthermore, high performers protect the brand both internally and externally. Internally, brokers want to work on a winning team that is constantly striving to improve.

Externally, a firm's reputation is reflected by the brokers on their team. Marginal brokers damage all the brokers."

TECHNOLOGY

As the team has evolved, so has their leveraging of technology. That doesn't mean Brad worships technology.

"If anyone thinks that technology makes our life easier, I suggest that they think again. Life was much easier a decade ago, brokers pretty much marketed their listings on Loopnet, and you had Costar or a similar service for research and data. Now there are so many competing firms for creating marketing materials, running the back office, marketing properties, obtaining demographics and data analytics."

Today, Brad estimates his firm spends at least seven times the amount it did a decade ago on these services. Some of the platforms PREP uses include Buildout, SiteSeer, Sites USA, Site to Do Business, Costar, Loopnet and Crexi. As for their CRM, PREP relies on a highly customized, shared Salesforce-based platform.

Brad was not a believer in social media for many years. He told me: "The industry is slow to adopt new technology, and spending a bunch of time on these platforms five years ago did not seem effective." Today, things are different. Leveraging LinkedIn and Instagram have been the platforms that have worked best for PREP, given their retail user and decision-maker target market.

Instagram is a natural platform for retail brokers, as is Facebook and perhaps TikTok. The lesson here is you need to be where your decision-makers are. Ultimately, like PREP, the dominant brokers become omnipresent, where prospects and influencers consistently see your content, and ultimately you become top of mind. When you reach the state of "omnipresent", your prospecting becomes much easier.

Brad notes, "This past year is the first year where so many people have said something similar: '*I can tell your company is doing very well based on what I see on social media.*' This feedback tells me that we are doing a good job utilizing these resources, but it also tells me that the audience using these resources has grown."

PANDEMIC

Like most profiled in this book, PREP's business benefited from the pandemic. Change is frequently beneficial to brokers. Here's Brad's review of the business impact of the pandemic.

"We spent the first few months of the pandemic listening to our clients, sharing information we had learned, and providing advice and resources when requested. Unfortunately, we witnessed many businesses close their doors. From our perspective, this increase in vacancy and the challenges our clients endured resulted in strong activity in the second half of 2020 and a record year for us in 2021."

THE FUTURE OF BROKERAGE

Brad has one of the best statements about how brokerage will change that I have heard thus far. "The role of the commercial real estate agent has changed from the person who had all the information to the person who interprets the information." Mic drop. Here's the rest of what Brad had to say.

"As we are bombarded by increased information, this role of an adviser, educator, problem solver, relationship manager, counselor, interpreter and analyst will continue to evolve. Selling, leasing, appraising and managing are all based on fundamentals. But then you bring the people into the equation with their own emotions, past experiences, financial objectives and risk tolerances, and what should be easy becomes quite complicated. That's why people need brokers who interpret, translate and advise."

BRAD'S TOP LESSONS

Brad thinks there are three important things he learned in growing one of the most successful retail brokerage firms in the State of California over the last decade.

"**I am a Sales Manager**. About ten years ago, I was having breakfast with a friend, and I said that I was 'sort of a sales manager', and he replied, 'No, you ARE a sales manager.' I now realize I can add value to my brokerage team through sales management and coaching."

Like many others in this book, Brad discovered that coaching and good management could be a force multiplier. In addition, he's learned that helping others achieve their goals is good for business.

"**Forecasters are Useless**. Any time you listen to someone prognosticating about what will happen, assume that they really have no idea. I have listened to so many predictions held by most industry professionals, economists and others that were simply wrong. As a result, I try not to put much value on any of them. Instead, I try to manage risk and my life satisfaction level."

Brad's in good company here. Professor Philip Tetlock of the Wharton School conducted a twenty-year study of forecasters and their predictions. His conclusion: **"the average expert was roughly as accurate as a dart-throwing chimpanzee."**

"**Corporate Retail Leasing Has Gotten Much More Difficult.** This type of leasing is much more difficult than in the past. The requests and demands of many of these retailers put a disproportionate burden on the landlord and frequently go beyond what is logical and reasonable. This results in numerous additional rounds of negotiation that should be unnecessary and fewer transactions being consummated."

As far as his superpowers go, Brad is clear on what these are:

"Company Focus: The fact that a high percentage of our business involves retail brokerage in Southern California's Inland Empire region is a definite lever for our success. Our team is known throughout the industry for this focus. In addition, this makes it much easier for me to manage the firm's resources to ensure profitability.

"Company Marketing: For the size of our firm, we dedicate a significant number of resources to marketing our listings, our company and our broker's success. This is about maintaining a high level of presence in the market since we know how easy it is for people to forget about you if you are not continuously reminding them that you exist."

Today, the processes and the analytics of your marketing efforts make all the difference in the effectiveness of marketing campaigns. A marketing manager must understand marketing messaging, lead generation, funnels, analytics and integration with multi-channel.

You don't need a highly creative person to lead your marketing department because creating offering memorandums, leasing brochures and proposals is not the most innovative work. Instead, you can outsource your creative needs. A few years ago, PREP hired a Marketing Manager who is more focused on processes and has strong technical expertise, which Brad feels has greatly benefited the team.

"Our Team is Home Grown: No one on our team had extensive experience as a full-time CRE broker working at another brokerage firm before coming to Progressive Real Estate Partners. Therefore, this is an opportunity to provide training and coaching to our team members that allows them to reflect on the PREP method of conducting our business."

And as far as the future for Brad, his goal is simple. Live a pleasant life.

LIVING A PLEASANT LIFE

"My #1 personal goal is to live a 'pleasant life'. For me, this is different than 'being happy.' I am not sure what it really means to 'be happy', but I think it is much easier to ask yourself at the end of the day whether you had a pleasant day.

"Regarding my brokerage activities, I am committed to only working with clients that meet three criteria. I must like them. The work must be interesting to me. And it must have a significant financial benefit. Working on an assignment that does not create a reasonable paycheck is counterintuitive to the concept of living a pleasant life.

"If I am working hard on something that does not have a reasonable amount of compensation, then there is clearly something else I could be doing that would create more pleasure in my life. (Second Mic Drop)

"Regarding Progressive Real Estate Partners, my goal is to maintain our boutique-style team-oriented structure while helping each broker be more productive by raising their personal income. I have no interest in adding numbers for numbers' sake. Instead, I want our team to have the best resources and support so they feel confident that they can exceed a client's expectations. As a result, we are constantly evolving through training, adding tools and building our relationships."

3 Key Takeaways

❖ Creative help is essential, yet it can easily be outsourced. It is the processes and the analytics of your marketing efforts that make all the difference in the effectiveness of your campaigns.

❖ The role of the commercial real estate agent has changed from the person who has all the information to the person who interprets the information.

❖ Do not work hard on something that does not have a reasonable compensation. There is clearly something else you could be doing that would create more pleasure in your life.

SAM DIFRANCO
TRINITY PARTNERS
RALEIGH, NC
THE DRIVER

Sam DiFranco brought his nickname, "Sammy the Bull", when he moved from Buffalo to Raleigh in 1997. The nickname didn't survive the move. After more than twenty years in Raleigh, he's just "Sam", and almost everyone who works in the commercial real estate arena throughout North and South Carolina admires him.

Sam lives by a motto he got from his parents. *"Giving is the hardest thing to do, but it always keeps coming back."* That is as simple as it gets when you are looking for a path to commercial real estate brokerage success.

This approach allowed Sam to build one of the most prominent brokerage firms in the Carolinas, Trinity Partners. It also afforded him the ability to build an impressive car collection that includes a Lamborghini, a Bentley, a Ferrari and his new Aston Martin. He considers them "garage trophies" and drives them regularly, most often to the office or the golf course.

Sam drove his Bentley to a recent dinner we shared while discussing this book. Sam loves his cars, but he never thinks of them as investments, despite their increase in value since he bought them. He says, "The only similarity they have with CRE is supply and demand for pricing, but one big differential to always remember is CRE BUYS THE CARS, never the other way around."

TRANSITION

Sam will be 65 soon and entering his 44th year with a real estate license. Today he's working more ON the company and not so much IN the company. We stress the ON/IN method in our coaching with CRE brokers.

When you do things that make the business run, you're working *in* the business. When you're developing strategy, creating systems, and doing other things to improve the business, you're working *on* the business. Working on the business helps you create a business where you get great results without having to do everything yourself. If you are unfamiliar with the ON/IN concept, I highly suggest you read Michael Gerber's incredible book *The E-Myth Revisited*.

Over the last eight years, Sam's company has grown from 16 employees to 63. Most of his personal goals have been achieved through a diverse portfolio of property ownership, along with a majority position within his company. His brokerage goals are limited to significant acquisitions and servicing a few select clients and partners.

Over the last ten years, Sam shifted his focus to building his personal portfolio and life balance with deal-making as the primary income source. He participated and invested in over 30 real estate transactions in which he is a partner. Sam sourced the deal, arranged the financing, assembled the equity investors and closed the transaction. On other occasions, he invested in a deal someone else sourced alongside other investors.

Sam has created substantial passive income from these investments. There's also a large amount of depreciation which he uses to obtain annual tax savings on his ordinary income. That lets him be more selective on the type and quantity of deals he works on daily.

Sam's immediate team comprises his youngest son Sam DiFranco Jr, now 32 years old with almost 11 years in the business, and another young man, Dylan Heafner. Dylan is 28. He started as an intern and is now in his 6th year of business. This dynamic duo complements each other's strengths and weaknesses. They still run complex deals through Sam, but his job is oversight and business development.

SPEED TO CASH

Sam also oversees a general brokerage team within Trinity comprised of an additional industrial/flex broker, an investment sales broker, a generalist, a medical sales expert and a retail advisor.

Due to their "speed to cash" concept, their team has consistently grown transaction volume by an average of 15-20% annually. The basic concept is simple.

If you find a deal that makes sense for either current cash flow or good upside/value-add, you will never have a problem getting money to buy and finance it. Historically in Sam's market, there has been a lot of money chasing, not a lot of deals. Sam and his team beat that by zeroing in on cash. Here's how Sam describes the process.

"We evaluate what deals we will work on and what we will say no to as it relates to how soon we can get paid. For example, when someone approaches us with a new development deal, either for sale or lease, we must determine when we will start getting paid. For example, a new ground-up development may take 18-30 months just to deliver a product, so by the time we get a lease signed or a sale closed; it could be 12 months to get the first half of the lease commission or 30 months to close and get paid on the physical asset."

Those are the kinds of deals that don't produce speed to cash. But, on the other hand, if they list an existing building for sale, they can close and get paid in 60-90 days.

Technology

When I interviewed Sam for Brokers Who DOMINATE, he was in the process of installing technology to help him keep up with everything going on in the market. Yet incredibly, Sam's team still lacks a functioning CRM more than a decade later.

How can that be? Many believe that technology is a key to success today, but there are exceptions to every rule. Sam DiFranco is an exception. Sam's exceptionally natural ability to network provides a continuous referral source for incoming business. Yet Sam admits, "if I had to do it all over again, I would have systems in place, a CRM, to touch my inactive and current clients so I wouldn't have to work as hard obtaining deals."

Sam has grown a successful business without relying on technology. Let's see what lessons we can learn from how he did it.

Sam hired a brokerage coordinator to help with researching target clients and sourcing common connections to them for introductions. His inactive clients, lenders and attorneys continue to be his source for referrals.

Building Business, the Old-Fashioned Way

Sam's reputation has continued to provide an abundance of work and leads. But don't be fooled into thinking that's easy. Like other successful brokers in this book, Sam worked his tail off and paid attention to marketing basics.

His business is built on referrals, and a key source of those referrals is inactive clients. That's consistent with Massimo Methods™. Sam constantly tells his team to stay in touch with their inactive clients. As Sam would say to you:

"The worst thing that can happen is you see a client that did a deal without you, not because they didn't like you, only because you haven't reached out to them in years and you were not top of mind; the tip of the tongue when they needed your service."

A solid personal reputation, impressive market presence and marketing basics have been keys to Sam's success. He doesn't expect the future to be much different.

THE FUTURE OF BROKERAGE

As you might guess from reading this chapter, Sam imagines a future where the basics of brokerage success will continue to be necessary. And of course, he adds his unique twist. So, let's hear what he says about the future of brokerage.

"Knowledge and experience will dominate. Knowing your market and your specialty and being able to solve problems for the clients will prevail. Providing value-added solutions and multiple options will be key. Also, efficient communications and follow-up will be essential with the ability to implement all the latest technology available but only used to the client's capacity without overkill. The ability to CLOSE will remain the most important thing while connecting the right people to do so."

That makes sense. What about Sam's unique twist?

"We decided long ago that we would become a 'marketing company' with an emphasis on real estate. Since most of the major companies tell their clients, 'This is how we do it,' we ask ours, 'how would you like this done.'"

SAM'S THREE LESSONS FROM THE LAST TEN YEARS

Here are the three essential lessons that Sam has learned over the last ten years:

"It doesn't matter how much money the deal is worth; if it makes sense, the money will be there. If you find a deal with good cash flow or good upside/value add, you will never have a problem getting money to buy or finance it.

"It's easy to insert yourself into deals if you bring value. For example, at some point we are all involved in a tenant or buyer rep situation. If you can show that client how their lease adds value to the landlord and take them to purchase for a later sale, leaseback, or long-term hold, you've added value. Now, if you take them from start to finish, you have a fan club to leverage for future work.

"Never underestimate who you are talking with or who they know, as they may be your next elephant deal. Make sure everyone knows who you are and what you do for a living. Keep it simple. I tell people, "I help people and companies buy and sell commercial real estate either for investment or occupancy."

Sam's superpower is that people like him. Sam is a goal-setting giver. Remember that advice from his parents? *"Giving is the hardest thing to do, but it always keeps coming back."*

Sam's a naturally nice guy who tries to help everyone he meets. If he can't help, he'll direct the other person to where they can get help. As a result, people feel good around Sam. So, they remember him and think of him when they're ready to do business or when they're asked if they know anyone in CRE.

Philanthropy is a perfect way for Sam to live out his parents' advice. He's passionate about giving and has a special passion for causes that help children succeed. Every year he volunteers time and donates to over fifty charities. That's a lot of giving and also a lot of meeting new people.

Sam says his success is all attributed to having and maintaining goals. He shared an example.

"I wanted to buy at least two properties per year for the past ten years, and now I have 30. The income stream from property ownership, brokerage and company ownership affords me a very nice lifestyle."

So, what does a broker who seemingly "has everything" do? Sam's future goals are as clear as his previous goals. He wants to leave a legacy within his company and continue to watch it prosper while slowing his participation to a few days per week. He is almost there. "I can see myself as the ambassador for my company and also doing more and enjoying my 18-month granddaughter, playing more golf, traveling with my wife and expanding my car collection."

Sam's success is a shining example of what can be achieved through commercial real estate. Some would say it is the American dream. But, for the Bull from Buffalo, it's simply a drive down south – with the top down, of course.

3 Key Takeaways

❖ Giving is the hardest thing to do, but it always keeps coming back.

❖ Touch your inactive clients regularly.

❖ Consider how Sam's "Speed to Cash" concept could impact your decision-making.

Caulley Deringer

Executive Vice President
Transwestern
Northern Virginia

The General

For the original Brokers Who DOMINATE book, I asked Caulley Deringer about the future. He responded with a favorite quote from Charles Kettering. "My interest is in the future because I am going to spend the rest of my life there." And what a "future" it has been for Caulley and his team.

When I wrote Brokers Who DOMINATE, it had been almost 25 years since I had seen Caulley. I met him in 1983 when he was the new hotshot freshman recruit for our Washington and Lee lacrosse team, the Generals. Caulley was as smooth and deliberate an attackman as I had seen, and he had a command of the field. He was indeed a general in the making.

Today, this has not changed one bit. Caulley now leads his team at Transwestern, and they dominate the Northern Virginia industrial and office landscape. They regularly complete about 125 transactions a year. Whether it's a 7,500-square-foot lease or the sale of a 14-building, 735,000-square-foot, $100 million industrial portfolio, the team is strategic with every client opportunity they have.

In Caulley's 35-plus years of real estate experience at Transwestern, he has leased and sold more than 29 million square feet throughout Northern Virginia. Additionally, he has executed more than 3,350 transactions aggregating more than $5.8 billion. He dominates his market.

Consistent as ever, Caulley started our 10-year catch-up with a quote from Oscar Wilde: "With age comes wisdom." Then he went on:

"I believe my personal growth over the last ten years as a broker has been through a deeper understanding and appreciation for what motivates and is important to our clients. My team pushes themselves to 'think' like our clients, which allows us a more meaningful understanding of their business goals which has us uniquely aligned with them as partners rather than clients."

That's the General strategizing his next move.

THE STRATEGY

Caulley would tell you that every client is different. Therefore, digging in to find their hot buttons is vital. Here are two examples.

They have one client who prefers to talk weekly about market trends more than about marketing the property. "She puts a premium on understanding the market dynamics to stay ahead of our competition. Providing her with the latest market scoop and statistics helps her to be more educated, effective, and responsive."

Another client, whom they have had for 20+ years, is entirely deal-focused and primarily interested in discussing pressing deals once Caulley's team has toured a prospect and sent a proposal. "We streamline the process for him by doing all the due diligence on a company's background/business and financial condition. We then present our recommendations and get a rapid response. Of course, it helps that this is a long-standing client who trusts us implicitly, but we have had the good fortune of a very successful track record by thinking like our owner and always keeping his best interest in mind."

The team strategy is different of course, for institutional clients. Asset managers outside their area often want to see and learn about the market. Caulley encourages them to come to town early and often, so they can drive the competitive leasing scene, see buildings that have sold and tour potential development sites. "We really enjoy this process because we believe an educated asset manager is better for the asset and its success. Following our tour or meeting is a great time to enhance a relationship with breakfast, lunch, dinner or another social event. Don't miss an opportunity to grow your relationships!"

Yes, Caulley the General strategizes how to work with the clients before, during and after each transaction. To reinforce his dominance in the market, Caulley and his team members work daily to become more efficient and effective. They proudly proclaim, 'We've become bigger, faster and stronger!' Indeed, with age comes wisdom.

Like a good general, Caulley places a premium on knowing the market inside and out and understanding the competition. What are other firms' best practices? Should they be doing the same? What should they change? The team repeatedly gathers during the week at set meeting times to ask themselves these questions and challenge their thinking. They also go on a couple of retreats a year to get out of town to brainstorm and strategize to define their short and long-term goals and how best to achieve them.

Beyond the transaction and above the commission, the team also strategizes on how to beat their competitors and get better. The team has defined intervals for review, reflection and repositioning their approach to the market and how to assist their clients better.

"We educate ourselves outside of our primary market. What are the national trends? What businesses are growing and where? What is the Federal government's influence? What is occurring in the economy that will impact our business, and how do we get ahead of it?"

A perfect example of this was the pandemic's effect on e-commerce growth. First, Caulley and his team encouraged their investment clients to pursue land and warehouse purchases before the tidal wave of demand. Then, with their existing building owners, they pushed rental rates earlier than their competition as they saw demand increasing and supply dwindling.

Caulley commands a marketing team to help retain their dominant position. "We often update our marketing pieces if they've been on the shelf too long and need new life. Our marketing department directly reflects our team, so we strongly encourage their positive collaboration and input."

Now is a good time for you to ask yourself important questions. For example, how old are your marketing materials? Do they demonstrate your competitive advantage?

Caulley also has access to an in-house market research team, which he thinks is one of the best in the business. "We are an information society, and as asset ownership has become more institutionalized and sophisticated, the demands for deeper and meaningful research are only growing."

Indeed, we are an information society, but as others have said in this book, it is not access to information that is a competitive advantage.

Instead, you gain a competitive edge when your presentation and materials use the information to position you as the authority.

THE TEAM

Two brokers are at the center of Caulley's direct team. Steve Cloud has been with Transwestern since 2010. He has completed 805 deals totaling $765 million. Andrew Hassett started in a junior role, but after eight years with the team he has grown steadily and matured into a very strong dealmaker- especially for landlord clients. That allowed Steve Cloud to focus on business development and expand the team's portfolio. Caulley describes how they work together.

"We pride ourselves on having a balanced attack, with each of us having different skill sets and strengths. I focus a lot on expanding our business and developing new relationships. Steve is detail oriented, works well with our existing clients, and is the leader of our tenant representation business. Andrew is very well-organized and a tenacious dealmaker with a strong appetite for growth. One characteristic we all share is a highly competitive spirit. We love to win and don't take losing well. We sometimes laugh about this, but our desire to win is a driving factor in our success."

TECHNOLOGY

Social media is an integral part of the team's marketing efforts. In addition to broker blasts and their Transwestern website, they use Instagram and LinkedIn to get the word out on projects.

For them, CoStar remains the leading information provider for the commercial real estate industry, and their advertising options offer a high market penetration to brokers and decision-makers. Beyond

Google and the parcel mapping systems of municipalities, the team leverages MapQuest, Regrid and AlphaMap if they need additional intel on sites.

When the pandemic hit, the team knew they needed to adapt even if they would only achieve short-term solutions. So here are a few things they did:

- They took videos of their listing vacancies. Then they sent them to prospects who did not want to tour in person.

- They significantly increased their contact with clients and did their best to educate them on what they were learning and seeing in the marketplace.

- They researched and invited their clients to interesting podcasts.

- They focused on more land development opportunities and repurposing underperforming asset classes. This early digging and homework paid big dividends in the last two years.

STRATEGY FOR A POST-PANDEMIC WORLD

As any good general would do, Caulley is spending more time understanding the pandemic's short and long-term effects on the team's clients and how the team can advise their clients in the world emerging after the pandemic. That calls for new strategies. Here is how Caulley outlined them:

"During the early design phases, when helping industrial developers with a new project, we work with the building architect, general contractor and engineers to ensure that market-appropriate ceiling heights, wide column spacing, ample truck courts, trailer storage, etc., are accounted for properly. Providing this information ensures that the right product is built for the market.

"We've examined ways to create better truck flow and increased parking opportunities in some of our older buildings with functionality issues. In addition, as land prices and building costs have escalated, we've offered strategic decisions to our clients to improve what they have. A perfect example has been the suggestion of increasing a building's ceiling height by removing the roof, raising the actual height and creating more cubic footage. These modifications have been a tremendous value add for landlords and tenants.

"On our office product, we work closely with our building owners and architects to think creatively about common areas and spec suite designs that accommodate tenants' desire for functionality and strong amenities. Of course, these also include design features that are sensitive to companies and employees with concerns about accommodating employees' personal needs in a post-Covid environment."

THE TOP 3 LESSONS CAULLEY HAS LEARNED OVER THIS PAST DECADE:

Don't be set in your ways and be willing to embrace an ever-changing commercial real estate world. Opportunity is everywhere!

Develop more profound, meaningful personal relationships with clients, which will allow you to enjoy the business more and keep clients longer.

Don't stop learning or growing. There is always a way to improve your game, no matter how experienced or successful you've become. You can always get better!

As for the General's superpowers —they're what you would expect from any true leader:

"I think like our clients and align my goals and success with theirs."

"I believe every deal can be made. Be creative. Be smart. Be hungry."

"I'm a competitor. I hate to lose and do everything I can to prepare to win."

As for the future, not surprisingly, Caulley relies on that exact Charles Kettering quote I referenced earlier. "My interest is in the future because I am going to spend the rest of my life there."

THE FUTURE

"My focus for the next ten years is to continue enhancing and growing our client relationships and focusing on the 'right' business pursuits. Of course, there is plenty of business to be had, but our pursuits will be with clients/partners that value and appreciate our skillset and pursue meaningful asset classes and transactions.

"I will make a more concerted effort to enjoy the business more. Our industry has many highly intelligent, interesting and fun individuals. I plan on spending more time enjoying the positive experiences of real estate and not letting the lows be as meaningful. Embrace the highs, appreciate the great business we are in, and don't let the tough times wear you down."

It sounds like this General has a good strategy for the future.

3 KEY TAKEAWAYS

❖ Think like your clients and align your goals and success with theirs.

❖ Consistently update your marketing materials – don't allow them to be a competitive disadvantage.

❖ Go beyond the transaction and above the commission. Strategize on how to beat your competitors.

DOMINATORS
IN
TRANSITION

DOMINATORS IN TRANSITION

So far, all the brokers we've covered have continued with traditional brokerage in one form or another. They responded to unique challenges, like COVID. They adapted to changes in the business and came up with new ways to succeed. But not every dominant broker chose that path forward.

That shouldn't be surprising. Everyone I interviewed for this book is creative and successful. They are constantly looking for new ways to get better results. It's only natural that some of them would choose a path different from traditional brokerage.

The brokers in this chapter are in transition. They're evolving and exploring.

BRAD AHRENS – EXPLORING NEW POSSIBILITIES

Brad Ahrens' chapter in Brokers Who DOMINATE was part of the "Young Guns" section. I described his first years in Phoenix when he tried different things as he learned what his passions were, what he was best at and what just didn't fit.

When we left him, Brad led the Ahrens Industrial Team at Commercial Properties, Inc. It looked like Brad's exploring journey might be over, but that wasn't the case. Here's how the journey continued.

In 2011, Brad brokered one of the largest off-market industrial transactions, the Phoenix, AZ MSA. That caught the eye of a national brokerage firm that made him an offer he couldn't refuse. At first everything looked good, but it wasn't really what Brad wanted.

At the end of 2012, Brad left brokerage to venture into his true passion of investment real estate on the principal side of this business. He founded BKA Equity Group to focus on acquisitions of undervalued industrial assets located in in-fill areas.

In 2013, Brad was introduced to a local developer in Phoenix who was working on ground-up senior housing projects. Brad's family had dealt with Alzheimer's and developing senior housing piqued Brad's interest. He rolled up his sleeves and created a joint venture with the local developer to deliver state-of-the-art projects that would create a safe environment for seniors, especially those with Alzheimer's.

Over the next few years, the joint venture developed more than $130M of senior and multi-family housing. Brad had found another piece of his puzzle.

Brad started Concord Development Partners in 2017 to bring his passions together. The firm develops best-in-class senior living communities and investment opportunities in Arizona and California's multi-family, industrial, office and retail properties. They have developed $85M of senior housing and expanded into several new asset classes with a continued strategy of ground-up development and acquisitions.

What's next for Brad? They say that past performance is the best predictor of future performance or success. If that's the case, then Brad's next step will be something that no one can predict, but it will seem perfectly logical once he makes his move.

CHRIS CHORNOHOS – PROGRESSING TOWARD HIS DREAM

Chris Chornohos was a natural selection for the "Young Guns" section of Brokers Who DOMINATE. He grew up working on his family farm on land that his great-grandfather cleared with a horse and a hand-axe after arriving in Western Canada from Ukraine. In his family, hard work was an inherited trait.

After university, Chris set out to tour the world. It took him a year supporting himself with odd jobs along the way. When he got back home, he made a list of all the things he might want to do as a career. He kept coming back to real estate.

It was almost an inherited trait. Chris' family were savvy real estate investors with a land and rental properties portfolio. He chose commercial real estate because it allowed him to "use my education, sales skills and the opportunity to create wealth."

Chris knew that an independent life was his calling, and he initially developed his commercial real estate skill set in appraisal. Later he moved to brokerage. That's where he was when I wrote about him. Since then, Chris has developed a synergistic alternative to pure brokerage, and for Chris, this meant learning new skills.

Chris joined a large general contractor to run their business development operation in Calgary. He leveraged his brokerage experience and previous contacts and clients to generate new business. Here's Chris' assessment of how it worked out.

"Trying something other than brokerage allowed me to learn how the construction process works and how to work within a larger team. I always knew that brokerage was a great foundation to learn the business and network, but my burning passion was to build, invest and develop real estate. It was always my dream to become a developer."

He didn't just dream about it. Chris built a small fourplex rental project that he still owns. Chris was getting a taste for doing his thing, his way, and developing real estate. Yet he wasn't done with making more changes in his career.

In 2019, Chris joined Newmark to help grow their valuation business in Alberta and across Canada. His focus is on multifamily and development land. The valuation business has allowed him to stay connected and continue working with several of his key clients.

While he's working at Newmark, Chris is also pursuing his development dream. He partnered with a longtime friend, a former commercial broker, and a former colleague from the general contractor company to develop an inner-city townhouse rental project. His appraisal background and brokerage experience give Chris an authoritative perspective on the market. Here's what he sees.

"I believe there is a fundamental shift in commercial real estate space, a confluence of forces is creating a massive opportunity within the multifamily asset class. I believe that Alberta and Canada are some of the best places in the world to own and develop real estate. That is why I continue to develop real estate on a larger scale, grow a real estate portfolio alongside my investors and help them live a sovereign life."

Chris' "sovereign life" echoes Brad Umansky's "pleasant life." Many other dominators don't have a name for it, but they set clear conditions for what they will do and whom they will work with as they create a new life.

ERIC NORTHBROOK – FINDING A CALLING

The first chapter in my first book, Brokers Who DOMINATE, was about Eric Northbrook. Let me remind you of his amazing story.

Eric learned the business by reading a book he got from his father-in-law, *Creating a Successful Career in Industrial Real Estate*. He combined what he learned with his drive and discipline to succeed at Sher Voit Commercial (now Voit), later in a partnership with Brian Driscoll at Colliers International and then at Cushman & Wakefield. He was one of the most successful brokers in the country, but on January 27, 2006 he was in a motorcycle accident that left him paralyzed from the chest down.

He went through 6 months of intense rehabilitation, supported by his wife, Denise. Making lemonade out of lemons, they established the HeadNorth Foundation to provide help and hope to families who suffered catastrophic spinal cord injuries in San Diego County. I donated part of the proceeds from Brokers Who DOMINATE to the HeadNorth Foundation.

Eric returned to work within seven months of his accident and had his most productive year ever in 2009. But that was also the year Denise was diagnosed with cervical cancer, and within 18 months, she passed away in August 2010. Eric pushed on and was focused on raising his two children, who were 9 and 11, when their mom died.

Eric remarried in 2014. That wasn't the only good thing to happen that year. 2014 was also the year he found his calling. Eric describes it this way.

"As the Executive Managing Director of Voit Real Estate Services, I am a mentor and coach for 50 people in the San Diego region." Leaning into his new career, he has increased team revenue by 275 percent over the last eight years.

Today, Eric is proud of his team's production, but when he communicated with me, he also mentioned people he mentored. He notes how successful they've become. He says, "I have raised kids coming out of college, and they are now married, own a home, and have children."

When he considers the future, he expects to mentor and coach his team and spend time traveling with his wife. He also plans to "Invest more into multi-family and single-family homes to create more mailbox money." That's a recurrent theme for the brokers in this chapter.

BOB BREHMER – A COMPANY OF ONE

Bob was the Managing Partner of NAI/Daus in Cleveland, Ohio when I wrote about him in Brokers Who DOMINATE. His story is inspirational and an example of what is possible, regardless of your circumstances. Bob traveled from orphanage beginnings to great success. Building on that success, he used the last decade to go where many brokers hoped to go.

Bob spends his days working on his personal investments and selecting clients he wants to work with. As Bob shared, "I've been reasonably successful, so money is no longer the primary focus, nor is market penetration and other measurable outcomes."

He only works on deals that meet two criteria. There is a minimum compensation threshold, and he must genuinely like the Principal and ALL their team members. That's where many brokers aspire to be, working on important projects with people they like.

Since Brokers Who DOMINATE was published, Bob transferred the day-to-day management of NAI/Daus to a partner and focused on his production and his portfolio of properties. At the end of 2018, the brokerage and management companies were sold to the new manager and an equity partner. Bob was required to stay on board for two years, more or less, "of counsel." He concentrated on his portfolio and a select group of clients who were transitioning from business to retirement.

Don't make the mistake of thinking Bob is taking it easy. He takes being called a "grinder" as a compliment. He's still seeking ways to increase his knowledge and value to his clients. For example, like Matt McGregor, Bob studies supply chain and logistics. He took classes "to brush up on my Excel skills".

When he looks ahead, Bob thinks that "Real estate is a local knowledge business." He doesn't expect that to change. He's also got a clear idea of what he intends to do.

"I will likely work at my current pace for perhaps five more years. I no longer have a company with overhead, financial obligations and emotional capital invested in my people. I have the flexibility to pursue whatever interests me, whether in my newly refined practice, my personal real estate investments or the companies I invest in.

God willing, I'll have plenty of time to fulfill my evolving goals and projects, but who knows how much time. Therefore, my time will be directed to those endeavors that provide the greatest 'Return on Involvement', such as work, charities and helping people new to the business."

Return on Involvement is a concept I shared with Bob during our coaching sessions years ago. It originates from the book *Relationship Economics by David Nour*. Life is not about money and analyzing financial returns (return on investment).

The most important element, and the one that can provide us with the great return of time, joy, fulfillment and yes, money, is Return on Involvement.

Bob is finding ways to use the skills and relationships he developed over his career. His shift from the day-to-day management of his firm to concentrating on selecting business seems like a natural progression. Tim Strange made a similar shift but in a very different way.

TIM STRANGE – DOUBLING DOWN ON PROPERTY OWNERSHIP

Tim Strange has closed over $1.2 Billion, that's with a "B," in sales and leasing transaction value over his 34-year career. He specializes in investment sales of properties throughout the U.S. For the past six years, he has focused on federal government-leased properties with the General Services Administration and Veterans Administration.

Since I wrote about him in Brokers Who DOMINATE, he merged his Sperry Van Ness brokerage with Grubb & Ellis and re-branded the company as Newmark Grubb Levy Strange Beffort, now, Newmark Robinson Park.

A turning point in Tim's career came in October 2013 when his best brokerage client invited him to dinner and played Jay-Z's *"Just Let Me Be Great."* Then the client said, "Strange, you aren't getting any younger, so you need to double down on property ownership."

Tim took that advice and has never looked back. Today he has $100 million in commercial real estate assets under management as Chairman of Rose Rock Development Partners. There's another $400M in the pipeline to be developed in the next 36 months. That may sound like he's abandoned brokerage, but Tim understands things differently. He says, "I will always be involved in brokerage going forward because of the relationships I have established and the synergism between brokerage and development."

Relationships are a key to success in our business. Bruce Lauer built an astonishingly successful career on relationships. He has set the example for a couple of generations of brokers.

BRUCE LAUER – THE BOSS IS STILL GOING STRONG

Bruce Lauer was my first broker. He pushed me to get better than anyone else in my brokerage career. Thus, his original chapter was appropriately titled "The Boss." The boss is still going strong.

He's 76 years old now. Every morning, he leaves his home in North Tampa at 6:00 am to commute down I-75 to downtown Tampa, some 23 miles south. Like many of the people I wrote about in my first two DOMINATE books, Bruce is a commercial real estate professional through and through. This is what he does, and to an extent, this is who he is. He loves it, and he works hard at it.

He works hard because building great relationships which great business success depends on takes time, effort and attention. He also works hard because, like many dominators, he knows you can outwork your competition.

Bruce admits his younger colleagues may think he's nuts. However, all those colleagues combined will likely never close the number of high-value transactions or create the number of high-quality relationships Bruce Lauer has.

Like all I have profiled in this book, Bruce's last ten years have been one of transition. In 2013, he sold CLW, the firm he founded in 1989, to two of his partners. The partners subsequently sold the firm to Cassidy Turley. Bruce admits this was a tough time for him. Here's how he describes the situation.

"I continued as an employee, even though I had no administrative responsibilities. It was difficult for me to sit and watch some of the decisions that were being made knowing I wouldn't have made them that way, but I had no say. They really didn't want my input."

This is a common theme for brokers who sell the firms they created, cared for, and nurtured over many years to a larger, much more bureaucratic organization. Bruce Lauer and Bob Knakal learned that aligning with a national firm comes at a cost. The big check that comes with the sale is tempting, for sure. But sometimes, in these independent to national firm sales, there is a question of what depreciates faster, money or freedom.

In 2015, DTZ merged with Cassidy Turley. Soon thereafter, Cushman & Wakefield came along and merged with DTZ. Many brokers were let go, but Bruce's position was secure. Bruce's personal and professional relationship with PGIM, Prudential Insurance's real estate arm, helped solidify their work and relationship with Cushman & Wakefield.

Here's an example of how Bruce Lauer brings in clients like that. Bruce decided to get involved in Morton Plant Hospital Foundation because it created an avenue for him within the hospital arena. The twenty-five board members were all senior executives from large regional companies. Each one is a potential high-value client.

You don't develop quality clients automatically simply by hanging around them. Bruce attended all the board meetings and participated where needed. In our interview, he stressed how important hard work and self-improvement are.

"In our business, you need to do that. I am not sure younger brokers appreciate this. I still encourage the younger people I work with to be part of Toastmasters, to learn how to present and speak."

I laughed at that one. Back in 1990, Bruce forced me to go to Toastmasters. I was scared out of my skin and shaking nervously with every speech. Of course, speaking in front of big groups is easy and enjoyable for me today. Thanks to Bruce for making me go!
Bruce Lauer is one of the Gamechangers I wrote about in Brokers Who DOMINATE. Gamechangers are brokers who have changed the way our current brokerage business works.

They have blazed paths for others to follow. The Gamechangers I profiled a decade ago were Jerry Anderson, Bruce Lauer, and Stephen Siegel.

You've read about two Gamechangers already in this book: Jerry Anderson and Bruce Lauer. Turn the page to learn what the other Gamechanger, Stephen Siegel, has been up to since the last time I wrote about him.

STEPHEN SIEGEL

CBRE

CHAIRMAN OF GLOBAL BROKERAGE

THE AUTHORITY

Commercial Real Estate Broker Dominators are authorities in an otherwise commoditized marketplace. They are sought out. They are resources. They are the consistent top producers. That's why this chapter about Stephen Siegel is profiled in this book's last and longest chapter. This icon of commercial real estate brokerage is, in fact, The Authority of authorities.

I was nervous the night before I was set to interview Mr. Siegel. It was Stephen freaking Siegel, the Chairman of Global Brokerage for CBRE, the biggest commercial real estate brokerage firm in the world! While I had the opportunity to talk with him some 10 years ago for my first book, and I met him in person during a networking function in New York City I attended about seven years ago, I was still anxious.

Many people in this book are CRE Rock Stars. Stephen Siegel is the Sinatra, Lennon, Springsteen or Lady Gaga of CRE, depending on your age and reference point. I have experienced the impact of Mr. Siegel's stardom myself.

When I was preparing to interview him, I sent out a tweet about the upcoming interview. That tweet went viral in the CRE space – well, as viral as a CRE tweet can go.

It seemed everyone knew who Stephen was or had personal contact with him. They all felt like Stephen was their best friend. Stephen Siegel makes people feel good. He has the gift of creating comfort and trust.

When I first joined the Zoom meeting for our 10-year follow-up interview, I told Stephen about my social media post and its reception, along with the incredible gratitude that was expressed and shared. Stephen already knew about it. Here's what he said.

"Rod, I want to share something with you. I got a call from a major client this morning from a big development firm and he said, "There was something on social media about you. And I got a whole bunch of calls. How people responded. About how good you are.""

Naturally, I wanted to know more. Personally, I don't use social media that much. I told Stephen I only have an Instagram account because my daughter challenged me to have it. Stephen didn't have an Instagram account. He said, "One of my guys showed it to me."

Ah, the beauty of social media! When done correctly, your interviewee feels that something is up before the interview itself. I clarified that I simply announced that we were having our 10th-anniversary book launch preparation. That this was the first of several steps in my preparation. Because he is an icon in commercial real estate, my post grabbed a lot of attention. Stephen put what happened in perspective.

"I appreciate you, Rod. That's great. It's very humbling. You feel like a king, and you come home and shoo bop; you're a court jester." Isn't that the truth for all of us? Even the icon of CRE understands that our professional success does not excuse us from our personal responsibilities.

The last 10 years

Stephen Siegel joined Cushman & Wakefield as a junior accountant at 17 and now has six decades of brokerage-related experience. He reflected on the significant changes in our business.

"The first leases and this is not a joke, were six-page leases for 100,000 square foot deals. That evolved over the years to greater sophistication. Real estate had been historically handled by the purchasing department. The head of the purchasing department, who was buying the pencils for the company, was also making commitments for tens of millions of dollars for the same corporation.

"Somebody in the C-suite realized, 'Holy mackerel, that's our second most expensive item on the expense line, the first being people!' That began to move up into the C-suite, if not all the way up, it went to the CFO and then became a whole different level of sophistication. That level of sophistication increased over time. And I guess in the last 10 years; it's transitioned even more significantly than I could have imagined.

"And the use of technology has, if you will, invaded our business. Everybody has got a new wheel that they've invented and a better way to do business. But frankly, it still boils down to the people, the quality of those people, and their ability to implement a strategy that's developed over time for a transaction.

"What's increased from a 10-year basis from what it was, is the requirements. I think the last time we spoke, I used the word 'demands', but it's not a demand. It's their requirement for the type of analysis that a corporation requires parallel to that strategic agenda, if you will. Where should they go? How should they go? And I'll get to the current tense because that's changed since the pandemic to some extent.

"And what is the best path for this corporation, not just financially, but how it impacts their people? We do zip code analysis and where the people come from, and how they're getting there. And what's the impact of that? Will they lose people if they move as little as 10 blocks away? I had a conversation with a major client yesterday in a meeting about deciding on locations, who said just that, 'If we move 10 blocks away, it changes the method of travel for 25% of our people. What transportation will they use? Seems like nothing, but that becomes a cost.'

"The type of analysis and the depth of it that corporations require in the last 10 years has accelerated by 500%. That's not an exaggeration. There's something called workplace strategy, where they determine what size every desk should be and where every workstation should be.

"There are corporations that dramatically increased their density per person, per space that they utilize. And frankly, there are others that go through that entire process, and they come up with 250 square feet per person going in, and they end up at 248 square feet. So, it was no change at all."

SELF-REFLECTION

Siegel acknowledges these changes are more obvious when looking at himself. "I'm a dinosaur. I'm sitting in a big office I fought bloody tooth and nail to keep; I have the desk that I had 30 years ago."

Of course, today, most CBRE offices around the country have gone to the open, more collaborative space. Even senior executives sit at a desk in an open area as opposed to a private office. Private offices are used for discrete meetings. In some offices, employees don't have desks of their own. They move from workstation to workstation.

They come into work, drop their stuff on an open workstation, log in, and that's their desk for the day.

In an ever-increasingly paperless society, Siegel is still holding out. His desk is hidden by stacks of paper, folders, and books. A set of blueprints in the corner and leases to be reviewed, client correspondence to be replied to. He jokes that "I've actually had clients say to me after Zooms, 'If you'd like me to stop by and clean up your desk, I'm happy to do this.'"

Siegel's grand desk reminded me of a picture I studied one day of famed Alabama football coach Nick Saban. The Massimo Group has become the biggest CRE coaching organization in the country, and maybe the world. So naturally I study coaches, both in business and in sports. Saban's desk was buried under playbooks, scouting reports, recruiting notes, likely fan mail, and maybe even some hate mail. But there is no hate mail on Siegel's enormous desk, just thank-you notes and gestures of admiration.

THE FUTURE OF THE OFFICE IN A POST-PANDEMIC SOCIETY

No commercial real estate market in the country was hit as hard by the pandemic as New York City, specifically the office leasing market. As I shared in the Knakal chapter, Bob could drive the streets of New York with little to no traffic while taking a complete inventory of buildings. He didn't have to worry about being delayed or interrupted. The New York City office market looked more like a post-apocalyptic landscape in one of my college kid's video games.

Siegel, unsurprisingly, remains a champion of office space. While he admits that his perspective, in some ways, doesn't reflect the reality of now, he strongly believes that people belong in the office. "The collaboration and the enhanced performance that you get out of people who exchange ideas and come up with one idea, another idea comes up with a better idea. Just the culture. There's no culture that can be built from home."

According to Siegel, corporations are demanding people return to the office. "The company that I was with yesterday is a major cosmetic company. Three months ago, they told their people everybody has got to come back. Now, 'come back' can mean three days a week, two days a week at home, but that still doesn't eliminate one square foot of space needed because if you come in for three days and somebody else comes in for three days, those desks all must be there."

Siegel doesn't believe an independent/flexible perspective on work is viable for an organization. He shared the story of a recruit he recently spoke with. "I talked to one last week who said, 'Well, I could start work at 11:00 and I can stop at 7:00.' And I said, 'What if I want you at 9:00? And I need you for a meeting? Well, there goes your 11:00. Are you going to work at 9:00 and take two hours off and work at 1:00?' Plus, now again, this person will not know any other person in the office. My advice is to get into the office and meet the people you are working with. And besides collaboration and culture, there is a social aspect to it."

ON BEING AN AUTHORITY

I shared with Mr. Siegel that we have something in common. He has coached thousands of brokers during his 60 years of professional CRE experience, and my company has coached thousands of brokers across North America (and a few, on other continents as well) ourselves.

As you can see from the many profiles in this book, the brokers who had the greatest success during the pandemic were seen as authorities by their clients. The brokers who were commoditized, seen by their clients as interchangeable with other brokers, did not fare as well.

Stephen is THE CRE BROKER AUTHORITY, so I asked him what distinguishes someone as an authority in commercial real estate brokerage. As usual, he had a provocative viewpoint.

"I think an authority is somebody who just doesn't sell; it's somebody who advises, it's somebody... I always use the expression that knows the company that they're either pitching or meeting with better than the company knows themselves. Knows every aspect of what happened, knows every aspect of what might be on the agenda toward the future, whether they're expanding, not expanding, what markets they're expanding in. And that broker that's sitting there and speaking to whomever they've been fortunate enough to get a meeting with, will just speak their speak. 'Well, I hear you did this. I hear you're doing that. You change your agenda to spread out your locations.' Whatever the case may be.

"For example, when I go into a tenant, I often say, and it's probably a little bit of an ego thing, I had fun my whole career. Before I even obtain the exclusive to represent, I sit with my people and say, "Here's what's going to happen." And I tell them where I think they're going to end up, and I tell them why. And that's because I've studied that company. I know what their needs are. I know where their people come from. I know how long they've been where they are, what it means with senior executives. Is there a history? And one particular company, I know the building they were in that they weren't leaving because the CEO's mother founded that company. And her first office was in that space and still intact as if she was still alive and running the business day-to-day. They were not leaving unless they could figure out how to move that office. So, it's knowledge, the key is knowledge of knowing who you're going to represent or would like to."

THE NEXT 10 YEARS

When forecasting the next ten years, Siegel quickly anchored his answer by referring to a lesson from the past. "It's funny. Somebody asked me a question the other day, 'Would you recommend your kid going into this business?' Because it's changing so dramatically, and brokers are being subordinated to some extent because of technology. I have been hearing that nonstop for 20 years. When I was with Insignia, our CEO Andrew Farkas was focused on moving brokerage to technology. Understandably it didn't work then, and the industry remains behind the curve today. "

Stephen continued to share that he feels technology is a tool, but to him, it's the experts that use those tools that will make all the difference. He admits that technology, just as in any industry, will eventually create a thinner number of people that are required because these tools allow you to serve more clients with fewer people. Stephen also feels there will be changes in fee structures.

Yet this business will never eliminate the people portion of it, according to Siegel. "A tenant, I don't care if it's a 1,000-foot user or a million-foot user, he's not taking space that he can't, or they can't walk and see and touch. That's going to be their home. So, I can give you all the virtual tours you want. What that'll do is narrow down where you're going."

So, the answer to that question about whether he would recommend his child go into commercial real estate brokerage. "Yes, I would recommend my kids, my son, my daughter, whoever to come into this business. The business will change. There'll be more technology applied, but the people aspects of it will not change ever."

3 KEY TAKEAWAYS

❖ Commercial real estate brokerage is a journey. Revisit Brokers Who DOMINATE and read Stephen's incredible story of the kid in the candy store who became the Chairman of Global Brokerage for the biggest CRE brokerage firm in the world.

❖ Gratitude will get you everywhere. Just be sure you are genuine and authentic.

❖ The world could use a lot more Stephen Siegels'.

Conclusion

"I am interested in the future because I expect to spend the rest of my life in the future."

~ Charles Kettering

You've reached the end of the book, but it's not the end. The future is in front of us, and your challenge is to take what you've learned from this book and your life experience and thrive.

I'm not talking about predictions. People have tried to predict the future for as long as we've been able to talk to each other. We've read tea leaves, cast lots, done extensive research and created sophisticated computer models. None of that really works very well.

It turns out that we only know a couple of things for sure about the future. We know that we cannot predict it in detail with confidence. We get it wrong, and the future surprises us. But we also know for sure that the future will be different from the present and the past.

In the past 10 years, we've seen a real estate tycoon become president and a health typhoon that brought commercial real estate to its knees. The health typhoon, the pandemic, was what Nassim Nicholas Taleb calls a "black swan", the surprise that no one expected.

LESSONS FROM THE PANDEMIC

During the pandemic, brokers split into three groups. Some panicked. They simply stopped all efforts to move their business forward and disappeared. Some were petrified. They didn't run, but they were lost, and they were stuck. Some wanted to help their clients, but they did not know how. Others had not developed trusting relationships with their clients.

A third group of brokers were proactive. The giants profiled in this book were in that group. They read, listened to and studied everything that was going on and became resources to their prospects and clients. They led the way. They dominated.

Mark Myers realized that his clients, senior living facilities, couldn't sell because no one knew how the pandemic would affect senior living. So, Mark and his team helped their clients get through by helping them acquire scarce equipment and stay informed about good ideas from other senior living facilities. In 2021, Mark reaped the rewards when transaction volume exploded.

Bo Barron saw the pandemic as an opportunity. His team doubled down on prospecting and marketing and made the COVID year their best ever.

Bob Knakal walked and drove the entire island of Manhattan south of 96th Street cataloging construction sites, vacant land and development opportunities. He built an incredible knowledge base that will help boost sales for years to come.

That's just a sample of how the giants profiled in this book turned a Black Swan challenge into an opportunity. There are two big takeaways.

First, none of the people in this book predicted the pandemic, let alone had a plan to deal with it. Instead, they assessed their situation and devised a strategy on the fly. When those big surprises come, it's too late to prepare. You must be ready.

Teams and businesses that survive a downturn and emerge stronger are the ones that prepare for bad times before they happen. There is a reason that squirrels collect and store nuts in the fall. They're getting ready for winter.

We know there will be bad times. Some will be like the pandemic, black swans that no one can foresee. Others will be business downturns. What goes up must come down. Always has, always will. We also know that you can do some things ahead of time so that you are ready when the hard times come.

You need four things to get through the hard times and come out stronger.

You need strong client relationships. When your clients trust you, you have more options, and you can move more quickly. This also includes your family. They need to support your commitment to brokerage.

You need resources to act. Several studies of economic downturns suggest that you need a strong cash position. If you're a spender, one that takes commissions and consumes, versus an investor, one who invests in themselves and their business, you will always be playing catch up.

You need courage. No matter what kind of surprise the future has for you, you will be in uncharted territory. Like the giants profiled in this book, you will have to consider your situation, pull your resources together and then act. Fortune favors the bold.

You will need confidence. Confidence in yourself. This can be very difficult in down markets. Market Dominators double down on effort, on marketing and on investing in their business. They come out stronger and with greater market share, as their timid colleagues evaporate, never to be heard from again.

LOOKING AHEAD

The world of commercial real estate has changed a lot since I wrote Brokers Who DOMINATE. It's probably a good bet that our business will continue to change and present you with new challenges. But don't expect everything to change at the same rate.

Technology will change rapidly. It seems amazing to me, but the FAA didn't allow companies to use drones for commercial purposes until 2013. Today, drones are common in commercial real estate.

Rapid technological change offers a lot of promise. Check out this definition of "proptech" from the software development firm, Dealpath.

"Proptech, or property technology, encompasses all residential and commercial real estate software. Various proptech tools and real estate technology platforms build efficiencies in different phases of the asset lifecycle, from deal management to portfolio management and beyond."

That sounds great, but as with many aspects of business, God is in the details. Your challenge as a CRE broker will be to sort out the good from the bad. Think about this warning from Ken Ashley.

"These tools can supercharge mundane processes and may save big money. But the wrong tool can be frustrating, expensive, and highly distracting."

As technology moves ahead you must find advisors you trust to help you make wise technology decisions. And you must learn how to use your tools to do business better. AI and systems like ChatGPT hold out the promise of making you dramatically more effective, but there will be a learning curve for you to climb.

Business and social norms will change slowly. There's a saying called "The 7 Last Words of a Dying Business" and they are *"We've never done it that way before."*

There's a kind of gravity that works on every business including yours. We don't like to have to change. We're comfortable with doing things one way and don't see any reason we should try another way.

That may have worked in the past, but those days are gone. Change is going to come as other businesses, like your competitors, implement better ways to do things.

As Matt McGregor suggested, you must stay about twelve months ahead of the curve, so you can spot changes that will give you and your clients a competitive advantage. You'll discover that the role of the CRE broker is changing. Brad Umansky described it well.

"The role of the commercial real estate agent has changed from the person who had all the information to the person who interprets the information."

That may be true in general. It's not true for everyone. There are brokers out there who are still doing business the old way. That's getting harder and harder. More and more brokers are adopting a long-term, advisory approach because it's what their clients prefer.

Human nature doesn't change. You, your clients, and everyone else want the same things. In addition to the basics of food and shelter, we want to control our lives and feel safe making decisions. We want people around us we can trust. That's why the basics of brokerage won't change any time soon.

You must prospect and build market presence. You must invest in building trust and long-term relationships. Those are the human parts of CRE. Software and AI can capture boatloads of data and deliver it at the click of a mouse and deliver it straight to your client. Only you can help your client make sense of it and make a wise decision based on it.

Turn back to Stephen Siegel's chapter and read how he knows why a certain client won't leave the building they're in. That's knowledge of the client and it's not something technology can provide.

Human nature is why we advise our clients to take a long-term, advisory approach to brokerage. Human nature is what can give you an edge. Stephen Seigel, the authority, says it well.

"The business will change. There'll be more technology applied, but the people aspects of it will not change ever."

There are challenging times ahead. It won't be easy. It takes confidence in yourself and conviction that CRE brokerage is the vehicle to build your wealth, to build your legacy. It takes hard work and staying on top of your game. You can do it. You're standing on the shoulders of giants.

Don't allow yourself to dissolve your practice into the sea of brokerage commodities. Position yourself as a market authority. Become a Broker Who Dominates.

ABOUT THE AUTHOR

Rod N. Santomassimo is the founder and president of the Massimo Group, the premier professional business consulting and coaching organization within the commercial real estate industry, in North America. The Massimo Group is proud to include commercial real estate professionals from some of the most accomplished organizations in the world, along with thousands of independent contractors, solopreneurs and small business owners in the United States, Canada, South America and New Zealand, among its clients.

Rod's career has consisted of several managerial and executive positions in private and public firms and several ventures in building his own organizations. He has been a featured speaker at a variety of local offices, regional conferences and national conferences, both in and aside from the commercial real estate industry.

Rod earned a Master of Business Administration from Fuqua School of Business, Duke University, in Durham, North Carolina, as well as a Bachelor of Arts in Commerce from Washington and Lee University in Lexington, Virginia.

Rod is a two-time recipient of the Duke University Fuqua School of Business Impact Alumni of the Year Award based on his work with graduate students and alumni to build a personal brand and creative approaches to secure greater client/prospect opportunities.

In addition, Rod has been recognized as a "Best CRE Boss" by AMI Media/Globe Street and was awarded a US Patent for his co-design of a sports workout watch.

Rod's first three books, *Brokers Who Dominate—8 Traits of Top Producers*, *Teams Built to Dominate*, and *Knowing Isn't Doing*, were all Amazon bestsellers. In fact, his last book, Knowing Isn't Doing, was the #1 Sales book in America upon its launch in October 2020. For more information, visit BrokersWhoDominate.com, CREteams.com, and Knowing Isn't Doing.com

Rod, a New York native, now lives in Cary, North Carolina, with his wife, Launa. The loves of their lives are their grown children, Giana and Nicolas. When Rod is not in his home office, you can find him running or cycling on the American Tobacco Trail, swimming laps in the pool or mostly throwing a lacrosse ball against a wall – always pondering "what's next?"

THE MASSIMO GROUP SERVICES

COACHING

The Massimo Group has the People, Processes, and Platforms to propel you or your team's commercial real estate business to new heights. In any coaching relationship, it is critical that you align yourself with someone who truly understands your business. The Massimo Group offers both group and one-to-one coaching programs for all levels of experience and expertise.

Our market-tested curriculum revisits best practices while introducing new techniques that will immediately impact your and if applicable, your team's production. Our commercial real estate clients consistently out-earn their agent peers by seven times!

By meeting 'face-to-face' with your coach via our video conference platform, together you will dissect your current practices and establish a personal plan for maximum production.

To learn more about how we work with our coaching
clients, please visit: www.massimo-group.com.

SPEAKING

You need to provide presentations that will attract strong attendance and participation and valuable and applicable practices and approaches for finding, winning and fulfilling business. Our presentations, whether for your local office or regional and national conferences, will captivate, motivate and educate. Most importantly, attendees will leave with tangible ideas and defined applications that will immediately impact their business.

To learn more about our speaking programs and to discuss your presentation needs, please visit www.RodSantomassimo.com.

EVENTS

The Massimo Group offers both public and private events, such as its highly acclaimed "Massimo Immersion," a 1 or 2-day workshop where attendees create their own customized Sales Playbooks with the help of certified Massimo coaches. In addition, our "MassimoCon" multi-day CRE brokerage conference is considered the best commercial real estate brokerage conference in the industry.

We also offer live, free webinars focusing on assisting commercial real estate agents and brokers in building the business and life they desire.

For more information, visit us on our social channels.

SOCIAL MEDIA

We are focused on providing value to the entire commercial real estate brokerage industry on all our social media channels. Please follow us:

LinkedIn - https://www.linkedin.com/in/crecoach/

Twitter - https://twitter.com/MassimoGroup

Facebook - https://www.facebook.com/themassimogroup/

Instagram - https://www.instagram.com/themassimogroup/

YouTube - https://www.youtube.com/@TheMassimoGroup

PODCAST

Subscribe to The Massimo Show. The objective of this business-oriented podcast is to share ideas on how you can maximize your professional and personal margin. Along with Rod Santomassimo, his guests will share how they find, win, retain high-quality clients and structure their business for greater freedom. To subscribe to the podcast, please visit RodSantomassimo.com.

BOOKS

All three of Rod's books were Amazon #1 Best-Sellers and continue to be commercial real estate community resources. All of Rod's books are available on Amazon.com.

Commercial Real Estate Brokers Who Dominate - This best-selling commercial real estate brokerage book has been the brokerage bible in the industry for the past 11 years. It was the basis for this book and shared profiles of a wide range of CRE brokers and their individual approaches to growing their personal practices.

Commercial Real Estate Teams Built to Dominate - This best-selling commercial real estate sales book outlines the specific steps for creating and structuring a high-performance team in commercial real estate. Like its predecessor, **Brokers Who Dominate**, this book outlines the practices of some of North America's most successful commercial real estate teams and dives deep into the science of assembling a high-functioning team.

Knowing Isn't Doing - This was the #1 Sales Book in America when it launched, as it outlines a roadmap to build the business and life you desire. Knowing Isn't Doing looks at every function of the building, running your personal brokerage practice, and transforming yourself from the sea of commodity brokers to a position of ultimate authority.

Made in the USA
Monee, IL
22 September 2023

43183725R00098